W9-DDR-083

"Good, no-nonsense recipes for meals that can be made in less than an hour."
The Boston Globe

"Dannenbaum's concept of preparation is that Italian cooking is based on simple procedures, using fresh ingredients and with respect for basic flavors."
The Philadelphia Inquirer

"Her recipes cover everything from great antipasti and salads to creamy risottos and marvelous pastas, to lovely and not too rich desserts.... I highly recommend her pizza recipe!"
Nancy Newman
The Chicago Sun-Times

"Julie Dannenbaum is a woman with tremendous flair and style."
James Beard

"From appetizers to desserts, ITALIAN FAST & FRESH provides dozens of dishes that are as delicious as they are attractive and easy to prepare."
The Suburban News

"The variety is enormous and it all seems so easy, so edible.... Put the book on your gift list and get one for yourself."
The Scranton, Pa. Tribune

JULIE DANNENBAUM

ITALIAN FAST& FRESH

BALLANTINE BOOKS • NEW YORK

Library of Congress Catalog Card Number: 83-48969

ISBN 0-345-33093-5

This edition published by arrangement with Harper & Row, Pub-
lishers, Inc.

Manufactured in the United States of America

First Ballantine Books Edition: April 1987

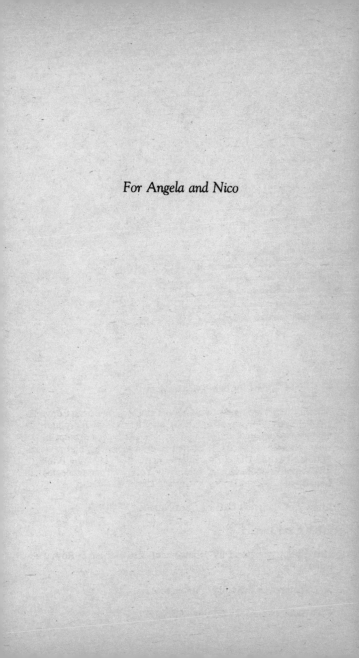

For Angela and Nico

Thanks to nearly fifty Italian chefs who taught me how to "cook Italian." Also, thanks to Massimo Alberini, food historian and journalist who taught me the history of Italy's cooking. Other friends to be thanked are: Arlina, Elizabetta, Natale, Connie, Aldo, Arnaldo, Guido, Nino, Fernanda, Stella, Franco, Bruno, Mario, Mauro, Lucia, Giovanni, Cesare, Theresa, Leonardo, Roberto, Pasquale, Luca, Giovanna, Pietro, Pina, Carlo, Giorgio, Lena, Sergio, Johnnie, Angelo, Dino, Lorenzo, Gino, Alberto, Ricardo, Clara, Anna Maria, Fulvia, Luciano, Carla, Gloria, Francesco, etc.

Contents

9. MEAT AND POULTRY   163

INTRODUCTION

ITALIAN FOOD HAS ALWAYS BEEN FAST AND FRESH AND as easy to make as it is fun to eat.

There are no complicated techniques, no difficult sauces, no mysterious kitchen secrets to master. Many people never get the hang of making a French omelet, for example, but anyone can make a frittata. Italian cooking, like Chinese, is based on simple procedures, respect for basic flavors, and good fresh ingredients. If there is one secret of Italian cooking it's summed up in a single sentence: DO NOT OVERCOOK.

We are not used to this kind of Italian cooking in America. Italian-American cooking uses lots of long-simmered, carefully tended sauces. There is nothing wrong with this food. It is part of our heritage—as American as apple pie. Or pizza. My first memories of Italian cooking are not of taste, but of smell. The smell of onions and peppers and garlic that filled the kitchen and the whole house of Mrs. Pellegrino, and sometimes spilled out onto the porch and crept up the hundred yards or so of street to mix with the much milder smells of my own mother's kitchen. My mother never used garlic, of course—like most Americans back then she believed that garlic wasn't really a flavor, it was a kind of halitosis in the raw. One sliver in a potful of food and the whole family would be doomed to a lifetime of offending.

My mother never changed her mind about garlic. But as I grew up, I learned to cook Italian, imitating as well as I could Mrs. Pellegrino and her wonderful heavy tomato sauce.

Then, nine years ago, I began spending two months of every summer teaching cooking at the Gritti Palace hotel in Venice—teaching and learning. Each year, well-known chefs from different regions of Italy visited the Gritti as guest lecturers, and they came like the wise men bearing gifts, bringing along their own knives, and some of their own special ingredients. Chefs from the seacoast brought their own fish and shellfish. Chefs from Genoa, where everything seems to be made with pesto or made to put pesto on, brought their own basil. They said basil outside Genoa was not good enough. A chef from Sicily brought his own lemons—lemons you could actually cut into sections and eat like an orange they were so sweet—and made the most magnificent lemon sherbet I've ever tasted I learned a lot about traditional recipes, and a lot about the new style in Italian cuisine called *nuova cucina*—a style similar, though of course Italians do not like to think so, to French *nouvelle cuisine*.

If this were a purist book, I would include only those Italian recipes that come from Italy.

But this isn't a purist book. First of all, I'm not a purist cook. I cook because cooking is fun—and cooking is creative. I could never leave a recipe alone, even if I wanted to.

And secondly, those good old Italian-American Pellegrino recipes are just too good to throw away. I've cut down the cooking time for the tomato sauce, eased up a little on the garlic, eased up a lot on the oregano, but I still make, and still love, things like veal Parmesan—which you'll rarely find in Italy.

Italian food, in Italy or America, is one of the healthiest diets in the world. It is high in carbohydrates from pasta, low in cholesterol because relatively little meat is used, high in fiber from greens and dried beans, high in protein from cheese.

And in Italy or America, Italian food is fun food.

Kids love it. At least, I've never met a child, no matter how fussy or finicky, who wouldn't take a second helping of spaghetti or another slice of pizza. And Italian food has the power to bring out the kid in all of us. You can't be formal, you can't be pompous, and it's very difficult to be totally serious when you're twirling pasta on your fork.

In Italy, I've watched hundreds of Italian families come into the restaurant for the traditional Sunday meal out. Father, mother, usually grandmother and grandfather, and two or three kids. They pick out a big table in the center of the room, sit down, pick up the menus—and decide to move. Mother or grandmother felt a draft on her neck, or the kids will be more comfortable against the wall. They sit at the new table, with a little fussing around they order, they prepare to eat. Napkins are tucked under chins, spread out neatly across large areas of chests, as seriously and carefully as if they were preparing for battle. The food comes. The wine comes. They begin to talk. Nothing serious—none of those desperate life-and-death conversations you sometimes are embarrassed to overhear in American restaurants. Italians keep their mealtime conversation as light as their sauces. They eat the food. But they don't just eat, they dine. They drink the wine. But they don't just drink, they quaff the wine. They have the knack of making a sip of wine an event, even if it's only from one of those squat little water glasses nine out of ten Italian restaurants provide you with. The meal is an event, too; an important part of family life. Mrs. Pellegrino would love it, and she would be welcomed with open arms. Her recipes would be welcome, too.

1

ABOUT
INGREDIENTS

THE REAL SOUL OF ITALIAN COOKING IS MAKING THE best of what's freshest and most available. Go out of your way to get the best and be sure to get what's in season. In recent years there has been an explosion of Italian specialty stores all across America. On my last book tour I met a young interviewer in Columbus, Ohio, oohing and ahing over a new local store that sold real Parmesan, real prosciutto, and real Italian olive oil. If you can get all that in Columbus, Ohio, you must be able to find some of it near you—no matter where you live. Although you can cook all the recipes in this book with American ingredients found in any supermarket, try at least to get these imported items:

Italian olive oil will change your cooking completely—and for the better. Italian oils are fruitier and tastier than American, and are smoother and without the bitter edge of the French oils. I use Bertolli for cooking—an excellent all-purpose oil. For salads, however, I use a dark green

1

and highly flavored virgin olive oil, Badia a Coltibuono, which has a rich, almost buttery texture. If you can't get Italian oils, at least try to get an olive oil labeled Virgin or Extra Virgin for salads.

Parmesan cheese, imported from Italy—not Argentina or Canada—is the cheese I use on pasta. Please, if you're asking me to dinner, don't serve locatelli, as it has a harsh and acrid taste, and the smell alone is enough to overpower every other flavor in any dish. The smell is not a good one—too sour to be appetizing.

Mozzarella cheese is rarely imported from Italy—it is too soft and delicate to ship. You can find good mozzarella in your supermarket, and in specialty stores you can often find a fresh homemade mozzarella, which is delicious. Smoked mozzarella, sliced thin and served with sun-dried tomatoes and a fine fruity olive oil, is becoming a fad appetizer in New York City's most expensive Italian restaurants. It tastes good, if a bit pretentious.

Flat-leaf parsley. I believe that if there is one ingredient an Italian chef cannot do without it is not garlic, but flat-leaf parsley. Is is obtainable year round, where it is available, and it has real flavor—unlike that papery curled parsley that's so pretty to look at and so insipid to eat.

Prosciutto. Italian prosciutto is wonderful, if you can get it. But there is also an American-made prosciutto, from Vermont, that is very, very good—and cheaper. Other American prosciuttos are too salty for me.

Though this is a fast and fresh cookbook, it is also an Italian cookbook, and I could not possibly exclude some prepared foods.

Canned tomatoes. For nine months of the year, these are better than fresh—if you consider those pink cottonballs we get in the supermarket fresh. Get imported Italian tomatoes if you can—those labeled San Marzano, grown around Naples and packed in Italy, are the best. Or get the best American brand available. I've had great success in freezing fresh tomatoes when they are at their peak. Packed whole in pastic freezer bags and frozen, they are perfect for sauce.

Boxed pasta. Italians used boxed pasta all the time—some sauces, especially fish sauces, are always served on it. Be sure to look on the side of the box and check that the pasta is made with durum wheat or semolina. Italian brands of pasta, such as De Cecco, Primo, and Rosa, are available in many supermarkets. These are extremely good—but if no one else in your neighborhood is cooking Italian, they can also get extremely stale. I have boiled and boiled and boiled old boxed pasta and never got it past the stage of slightly crunchy leather. You will know old pasta when you try to cook it. You can tell very old pasta by looking closely at it—it will be mottled with white dots. I don't know why that happens, but it means that something is breaking down in the pasta and it means you should buy something else.

Italian tuna. This comes in cans—and tastes better than fresh. It is dark, flavorful, and packed in a heavy olive oil. American canned tuna is not a substitute. Get this or make another recipe.

Anchovies. You can get salted anchovies to clean and store in olive oil at home, if you have a good specialty store near you. Otherwise, a good brand packed in those tiny cans will work fine.

Vinegar. Balsamic vinegar from Modena is extremely popular in America. For me it is too sweet and pungent. I much prefer the Sasso brand of red or white wine vinegar. A little goes a very long way.

Fresh garlic is most important for good flavor. I bring strings of it home from Italy each August, and hang it on a nail in my kitchen. Even after using it all winter long, I find what's left is still firm and juicy by spring. Much better than any I can buy in my markets.

Tomato paste that comes in a tube is much more economical than paste from a can. Simply squeeze out the amount needed and cap the tube and refrigerate until needed again.

Herbs. Use fresh herbs when available. Grow your own, or have a friend grow them for you. Basil is the herb I use most frequently. To have fresh basil flavor in my sauces in the winter, I purée basil leaves with olive oil, either in the blender or food processor. Place in a jar and keep in the refrigerator for a few weeks, or freeze in ice cube trays.

2

APPETIZERS AND SALADS

THERE ARE FRIENDS OF MINE WHOSE EYES MIST UP AND go dreamy when they talk about dessert carts in expensive French restaurants. Any conversation about food, no matter how it starts, is sooner or later worked around to extravagant mounds of whipped cream, floating island, rolls of confectioners' chocolate and shiny little tarts made of fruit laid out in geometrical designs.

I feel exactly the same way—about the antipasto display in the restaurants in Italy. One of the wonderful things about Italian food is the colors it uses: purple eggplant, bright red tomato, yellow lemon, green zucchini, dark green spinach, pale melon, and dark red prosciutto. Italians arrange their antipasto table with the same care and the same eye for design that the French put into the dessert cart—down to those tiny eggplants, sliced lengthwise to the blossom end and then opened out into a perfect little fan shape, as geometrical and as pretty as any fruit tart.

In Italy, it is better not to order antipasto—that's like

5

ordering entree. Just take a look at the table and select
what you want: grilled eggplant; spinach sautéed in olive
oil and garlic; shrimp dressed with lemon; mozzarella
tossed in olive oil and hot peppers; or something as simple
and delicious as radishes and crunchy bread.

There's nothing wrong with American-style antipasto,
of course. But you shouldn't feel that every guest has to
get one little smidge of fifteen different ingredients. Anything can be antipasto—whatever is colorful, light, and
good to eat.

Included in this section are ten pasta salads. A pasta
salad is an American food fad that tastes good enough to
last awhile. I think. Don't blame me if it is outdated before
your next dinner party, though.

Toasted Bread and Cheese with Anchovy Sauce

Anchovies packed in salt may be used here, if available.
Be sure to wash them very well, split them open to remove
the bone, and wash again. Anchovies in a can are perfectly
acceptable.

*1 long loaf day-old
    Italian bread
1 pound Fontina cheese
¼ pound butter, melted
½ teaspoon chopped
    fresh oregano
2 cans (2 ounces each)
    flat anchovy fillets,
    drained and chopped*

*½ cup olive oil
2 garlic cloves, finely
    chopped
2 tablespoons chopped
    flat-leaf parsley
¼ cup red wine vinegar*

1. Cut the bread into 2-inch squares. Cut the cheese into
   1-inch cubes. Beginning and ending with bread, alternate bread and cheese on 8-inch skewers.
2. Lay the skewers on a buttered baking dish and drizzle
   melted butter over each. Sprinkle with oregano. Bake

at 350 degrees until the cheese melts and the bread begins to toast, 10–15 minutes.

3. Meanwhile, mash the anchovies in a small saucepan and add the oil, garlic, parsley, and vinegar. Heat until the mixture bubbles.

4. To serve, slip the bread and cheese off the skewers onto individual plates. Pour the sauce over. Serves 6–8.

Parsley or Basil Paste

Spread this mixture on day-old slices of bread and toast in the oven. Or serve with bread sticks. It is also good as a sauce for pasta.

1 small bunch flat-leaf parsley, or 1 cup finely chopped fresh basil
12 tablespoons butter

4 scallions, chopped
Juice of ½ lemon
Salt and fresh pepper to taste

1. Chop the parsley by hand or in a food processor.
2. Soften the butter by beating it with a wooden spatula in a bowl, or cream it in a mixer or food processor. Combine with the parsley, scallions, lemon juice, salt, and pepper. Pack into a small crock or bowl. Makes 1½ cups.

Fried Mozzarella

Served with a salad, this can be a light lunch.

1 pound mozzarella cheese, cut into finger-size sticks
½ cup flour

2 eggs, slightly beaten
1 cup dry bread crumbs
Oil for frying

1. Roll the sticks of cheese in the flour. Dip in beaten egg and roll in bread crumbs. Place on a rack over a baking sheet and chill in the freezer 10–15 minutes.
2. Heat 2 inches of oil in a skillet. When hot, fry the cheese, a few pieces at a time, until brown. Drain on brown paper. Serve hot. Serves 4–6.

Mortadella with Vegetables

8–10 slices mortadella
1 cucumber, peeled
  and thinly sliced
6 tomatoes, sliced

½ cup black or green
  olives
Oil and vinegar in
  cruets

Overlap slices of mortadella around the edge of a serving platter. Alternate slices of cucumber and tomato in the center and decorate with olives. Serve with crusty bread or bread sticks and pass the oil and vinegar. Serves 4–6.

Gorgonzola Mousse

I serve this with drinks or as a cheese course with salad.

¾ pound butter, at room
  temperature
1 pound Gorgonzola
  cheese at room
  temperature
3 tablespoons red wine

1 tablespoon chopped
  flat-leaf parsley
½ teaspoon hot pepper
  flakes
1 tablespoon vegetable
  oil

1. Place the butter in a mixer bowl or food processor. Beat until creamy.
2. Add the Gorgonzola cheese and beat until well blended and light. Add the wine, parsley, and pepper flakes and blend well.

3. Oil a 5-cup loaf mold and pour the mixture into the mold. Smooth the top with a spatula and bang down a few times. Set in the freezer ½ hour to chill rapidly.
4. Unmold and serve with toasted bread. Makes 12–16 servings.

Note: This mixture can be placed in a crock and served immediately.

Bruschetta

I think this is the forerunner of garlic bread, which you can find in French restaurants, Italian restaurants, and steak houses throughout the United States—but nowhere else in the world.

1 loaf Italian bread
  (country loaf)
  Garlic cloves, mashed
1 cup olive oil

Coarse salt and fresh
pepper to taste
(optional)

1. Cut the bread into thick slices. Toast each slice of bread under the broiler or over a charcoal grill.
2. Rub each piece while hot with garlic.
3. Place bread on a serving dish and pour the olive oil over. Sprinkle with coarse salt and fresh pepper, if desired. Serves 4–6.

Variation

Lay the bread on a serving platter in one layer. Mix together finely chopped tomato and arugula. Moisten with olive oil and sprinkle over the bread. Eat for lunch.

Stanley's Salami Wafers

Make more of these than you think you will need as they disappear quickly.

1 pound salami in a roll

Remove the casing from the salami. Cut salami into paper-thin slices and lay on a baking sheet. Place in a 400-degree oven and bake until all the fat melts away and the slices curl at the edges. Serve hot or cold with drinks. Serves 4–6.

Bagna Caôda

This dip for vegetables will stay warm if the pot is placed over a candle or Sterno flame.

4 tablespoons butter
8 anchovy fillets,
  chopped
1 garlic clove, chopped
2 cups heavy cream

White truffles (optional)
An Assortment of raw
  vegetables
½ teaspoon potato flour
  or arrowroot

1. In a fondue pot, melt the butter and add the anchovies and garlic. Stir until the anchovies are melted.
2. Add the heavy cream and heat without boiling.
3. To prevent the mixture from separating, place the potato flour or arrowroot in a small bowl and whisk it with 1 tablespoon of cream or water. Gently whisk into the hot mixture. Slice or grate white truffle, as much as your budget will bear, and stir in.
4 Serve as a dip with raw vegetables, such as carrot sticks, baby artichokes, cardoons, celery, fennel, scallions, red or green pepper strips, etc. Bread sticks are nice to serve here. Serves 4–6.

Stuffed Shells

Try these shells as appetizers or use the fillings for sandwiches. They stay put and are much more pleasant than those gooey little sandwiches that always seem to ooze out their contents on everybody's fingers. You can use the same fillings spooned over fish or vegetables, or tossed with hot pasta.

16 large shell pasta,
   cooked

Rinse the shells with cold water to chill rapidly. Place the shells in salad spinner to dry. Place on towels. Fill each shell with 1 tablespoon of any filling desired and serve with drinks. Makes 16.

Anchovy Butter

12 tablespoons butter,
   softened
¼ cup anchovy fillets,
   drained

Juice of ½ lemon
2 tablespoons chopped
   flat-leaf parsley
Fresh pepper to taste

Mix all the ingredients in a bowl and beat with a wooden spatula until creamy, or blend in a food processor. Spoon into shells. Place in the refrigerator for 15 minutes. Makes filling for 16 shells.

Gorgonzola Cheese Butter

½ cup Gorgonzola
   cheese, at room
   temperature
¼ pound butter,
   softened

Fresh pepper to taste
2 tablespoons very finely
   chopped scallions

Mix all the ingredients in a bowl and beat with a wooden spatula until creamy, or blend in a food processor. Spoon into shells. Place in the refrigerator for 15 minutes. Makes filling for 16 shells.

Olive Butter

12 tablespoons butter,
    softened
¼ cup pitted and
    chopped black olives

1 tablespoon grated
    onion
Fresh pepper to taste

Mix all the ingredients in a bowl and beat with a wooden spatula until creamy, or blend in a food processor. Spoon into shells. Place in the refrigerator for 15 minutes. Makes filling for 16 shells.

Prosciutto and Fruit

2 large cantaloupes,
    Persian melons,
    Spanish melons,
    honeydew, or whatever
    is available

½ pound prosciutto,
    sliced paper thin
Lemon wedges

Cut the melon into thin slices, removing the rind. Arrange 3 or 4 slices of melon on each plate and cover each slice with a thin slice of ham. Garnish with lemon wedges and pass a pepper mill. Serves 6.

Note: Instead of melon, substitute fresh ripe pears or use figs, peeled, when in season. Occasionally, I serve the fruit with thin slices of well-flavored salami.

Grilled Melon and Prosciutto

1 ripe melon, preferably
  cantaloupe
4 tablespoons honey
2 tablespoons mustard
2 tablespoons red wine
  vinegar

Salt and fresh pepper
  to taste
½ pound thinly sliced
  prosciutto

1. Peel the melon and cut it into 1-inch cubes. Place in a bowl.
2. Mix together in a small bowl the honey, mustard, vinegar, salt, and pepper. Pour over the melon and mix gently. Let stand 10–15 minutes.
3. Cut the prosciutto into quarters and wrap each melon cube with a piece of prosciutto. Place on small skewers. Put them 2 inches from the broiler unit for 1 or 2 minutes to heat through. Serves 6.

Note: These may also be served cold, without broiling them.

Mixed Antipasto

2 peppers, one green
  and one red, if
  possible, seeded and
  thinly sliced
4 medium tomatoes,
  sliced

3 hard-cooked eggs,
  peeled and sliced
½ cup black or green
  olives
Oil and vinegar in
  cruets

Arrange the vegetables and eggs decoratively over-lapped on a platter and top with olives. Pass the cruets of oil and vinegar. Serve with crusty bread slices, bread sticks, or bruschetta (see page 9). Serves 4–6.

Bananas with Prosciutto

This is something like banana and bacon fritters, reduced to essentials, and turned into very good finger food. A good appetizer, and great with drinks.

6 bananas, not overripe
¼ pound thinly sliced
    prosciutto

1 cup freshly grated
    Parmesan cheese
Olive oil for frying

1. Peel and cut the bananas into 2-inch pieces. Cut the prosciutto into 2-inch-wide strips. Wrap each piece of banana with prosciutto. Secure with toothpicks. Roll in Parmesan cheese.
2. Heat 2 inches of oil to 350–360 degrees. Add the prepared banana pieces. Fry to just light golden brown, 2–3 minutes. If fried too long the cheese will burn. Drain on absorbent paper. Remove toothpicks. Serves 6.

Pickled Eggplant

1 large eggplant, cut
    into 1½-inch cubes,
    unpeeled
1 garlic clove, chopped
½ cup red wine vinegar
1 teaspoon oregano,
    chopped

Salt and fresh pepper
    to taste
1 cup olive oil
1 teaspoon finely
    chopped mint

1. Drop the eggplant cubes into boiling water to cover and cook over moderate heat 5–10 minutes. The eggplant should remain firm. Drain and place in a bowl.
2. Combine the remaining ingredients in a small bowl and pour over the eggplant. Toss well to combine. Serves 4–6.

Note: A few capers can be added to the dressing. Cooked carrots or onions may also be prepared in this manner.

Eggplant Relish Salad

I'm not convinced that salting eggplant to draw off its liquid really removes the bitterness. I think parboiling or deep frying for 1 minute is just as effective, and quicker.

2 medium eggplants
¾ cup olive oil
1 pound ripe tomatoes, peeled, seeded, and chopped
2 celery ribs, chopped
½ cup sliced black olives

2 tablespoons capers
2 tablespoons red wine vinegar
Salt and fresh pepper to taste
½ cup toasted pine nuts (see note)

1. If the eggplant is young, do not peel it. Cut into 1-inch cubes. Parboil or deep fry the cubes for 1 minute. Rinse, drain, and dry the eggplant.
2. Heat ½ cup olive oil in a large sauté pan and brown the eggplant, stirring with a wooden spatula, 5 to 10 minutes. Remove with a slotted spoon to a large bowl.
3. Add the remaining oil to the pan. When hot, add the tomatoes and celery. Cover and cook over low heat 10 minutes.
4. Add the olives, capers, vinegar, salt, pepper, and sautéed eggplant and cook, uncovered, 10 more minutes, stirring occasionally. Toss with the pine nuts and serve hot or at room temperature. Serves 6.

Note: To toast pine nuts, lay them on a baking sheet. Bake 10 minutes at 350 degrees.

Mixed Vegetable Relish

½ cup olive oil
4 tablespoons white
  vinegar
1 garlic clove, chopped
  Salt and fresh pepper
  to taste
1 cup shredded carrot

1 cup chopped green
  pepper
1 cup chopped celery
½ cup sliced pitted ripe
  olives
½ cup sliced pimiento-
  stuffed olives

1. In a small bowl, combine the oil, vinegar, garlic, salt, and pepper. Stir to mix well.
2. Combine the remaining ingredients and pour the dressing over the mixture. Toss to coat lightly. Refrigerate until ready to serve. Stir several times during chilling. Makes 4 cups.

Tomatoes and Anchovies

6 large tomatoes, peeled
  and sliced
2 small cans anchovy
  fillets, rinsed and
  dried, or anchovies
  packed in salt

1 tablespoon capers,
  rinsed and dried
Juice of 1 lemon
Fresh pepper to taste
Olive oil (optional)

Arrange the sliced tomatoes on a serving platter. Place the anchovy fillets on the tomato slices. Sprinkle the capers over the top. Squeeze the lemon juice over and grind fresh pepper over surface. Sprinkle with olive oil, if desired. Serves 4–6.

Fennel with Oil and Lemon

4–5 bulbs of fennel,
    bases, feathery
    tops, and coarse
    outside layer
    removed
Juice of 1 lemon

Salt and fresh
    pepper to taste
½ cup olive oil
1 tablespoon chopped
    fennel tops

Cut the fennel into small thin strips. Put into a salad bowl. Squeeze the lemon juice over. Season with salt and pepper and add the olive oil. Toss to combine. Garnish with chopped fennel tops. Serves 4–6.

Variations

1 small head chicory,
    washed and cut into
    bite-size pieces
2–3 anchovy fillets,
    drained and
    chopped, or
    anchovies packed in
    salt

1 hard-cooked egg,
    chopped

1. Fennel with chicory. Add the chicory, chopped anchovies, and egg to fennel with oil and lemon.
2. Fennel with capers. Add 1 tablespoon capers to fennel with oil and lemon (above).
3. Fennel with mozzarella. Add 1 cup mozzarella cut into matchstick slices to fennel with oil and lemon.

Sweet Pepper Salad

This salad is delicious and crunchy. It is particularly attractive made with red and green peppers.

2 cups finely sliced
  celery
3 peppers, seeded and
  finely diced
1 red onion, peeled and
  finely chopped
  Salt and fresh
  pepper to taste

2 tablespoons red
  wine vinegar
6 tablespoons olive oil
2 tablespoons
  chopped flat-leaf
  parsley

Combine the vegetables in a serving bowl. Pour over the remaining ingredients. Toss well and marinate 30 minutes if there is time. Serves 6.

Fresh Tuna Salad

2½ pounds fresh tuna,
  cut into finger-size
  strips
1 garlic clove,
  chopped
  Juice of 2 lemons
½ cup olive oil
2 tablespoons chopped
  fresh basil
  Salt and fresh pepper
  to taste

¼ cup dry Marsala
  Lettuce leaves, torn
  or cut into bite-size
  pieces

1. Lay the tuna strips on a baking sheet.
2. Mix together the garlic, lemon juice, oil, basil, salt, pepper, and Marsala. Spoon the mixture over the fish. Place the baking sheet in a 350-degree oven. Bake 7–10 minutes, or just until fish flakes.
3. Serve warm on lettuce with the juices spooned over. Serves 4–6.

Variation

Instead of tuna, use any available fish—salmon, swordfish, etc. Bake 7–10 minutes, till fish barely flakes.

Italian Tuna Salad

Be certain to buy tuna that says "packed in Italy" on the can.

½ cup olive oil
½ cup lemon juice
2 tablespoons chopped
  capers
  Salt and fresh pepper
  to taste
3 to 4 basil leaves,
  chopped
½ teaspoon chopped
  fresh oregano

2 cups sliced zucchini
1 can (13 ounces) tuna,
  drained and flaked
1 bunch scallions, cut
  into ½-inch pieces
½ cup sliced pitted black
  olives
½ pound cooked shells
  or macaroni

1. To make the dressing, whisk together the oil, lemon juice, capers, salt, pepper, basil, and oregano.
2. In a large bowl, combine the remaining ingredients. Pour the dressing over and toss lightly until the pasta mixture is evenly coated. Serves 6.

Flounder Fillets Cooked in Oil and Vinegar

Flounder is the easiest fish to find in the market; year in and year out, no matter what the season, it's always there. This recipe lets the tart taste of vinaigrette dressing go right into the fish, giving it a bright new taste.

4 tablespoons red wine
  vinegar
1 teaspoon Dijon
  mustard
  Salt and fresh pepper
  to taste
¾ cup olive oil
6 very small flounder
  fillets, cut lengthwise
  into 2 pieces

¾ cup pitted black olives
1 small head romaine,
  cut into bite-size
  pieces
2 tablespoons chopped
  flat-leaf parsley

1. In a small bowl, whisk together the vinegar, mustard, salt, and pepper. Add the oil slowly and whisk until the mixture thickens slightly.
2. Place the fish on a flat, heatproof platter. Top with a bit of the oil and vinegar mix. Bake at 400 degrees for 3–4 minutes, or until the fish barely flakes.
3. Meanwhile, place the olives, romaine, and parsley in a large bowl. Add the remaining dressing and toss. Spoon onto six salad plates and arrange two pieces of fish on each salad. Serve immediately. Serves 6.

Wilted Salad with Shrimp

Salad greens, such as
  arugula, radicchio,
  and Boston lettuce
1 pound baby shrimp,
  cooked and cleaned
2 small zucchini,
  julienned

Salt and fresh pepper
  to taste
½ medium black truffle,
  fresh or tinned
½ cup dry vermouth
12 tablespoons butter

1. Arrange salad greens on individual salad plates. Divide the shrimp among the plates. Arrange some zucchini

on each plate. Season each serving with salt and pepper. Keep at room temperature.

2. Chop the truffle and put into a small saucepan. Add the vermouth and cook over a medium flame to reduce to 2 tablespoons of liquid with the truffle. Start adding the butter, a little at a time, as for beurre blanc. The mixture should be creamy.

3. Pour some truffle butter over each salad and serve. Serves 4–6.

Shrimp, Potato, and Egg Salad

Lettuce leaves
1 pound cooked medium shrimp, peeled
4 large cooked potatoes, peeled
4 hard-cooked eggs, peeled

¾ cup chopped celery
¼ cup chopped flat-leaf parsley
Salt and fresh pepper to taste
6 tablespoons olive oil
3 tablespoons wine vinegar

1. Line a salad bowl with lettuce leaves. Add the shrimp.
2. Cut the potatoes into cubes and quarter the eggs. Place in the salad bowl and add celery, parsley, salt, and pepper.
3. Blend the oil and vinegar separately in a small bowl and add to the salad. Toss lightly. Serves 4–6.

Market Salad

All of the ingredients in this salad must be very fresh and ripe.

2 cucumbers, seeded
   and diced
1 head Bibb lettuce, cut
   into small pieces
1 small head radicchio,
   cut into small pieces
1 bunch arugula, cut
   into small pieces
3 celery ribs, finely
   chopped
3 ripe tomatoes, peeled,
   seeded, and chopped

1 small cantaloupe,
   diced
1 apple, peeled and
   diced
8 mushrooms, thinly
   sliced
¼ cup vinegar
⅔ cup olive oil
   Salt and fresh pepper
   to taste

Mix all the vegetables and fruits together in a large salad bowl. Pour the vinegar and oil over and season with salt and pepper. Toss well. Serves 6–8.

Salad Valentino

This simple and delicious salad is one I learned from studying with Valentino Marcattilii, chef of the famous San Domenico restaurant in Imola, just outside Bologna. He is a very special chef and I think this is a super special salad.

1 small head radicchio
1 small head Bibb
   lettuce
1 small head Boston
   lettuce
½ pound thinly sliced
   prosciutto
4 tablespoons butter
3 tablespoons red wine
   vinegar

2 hard-cooked eggs,
   whites only, chopped
2 tablespoons water
1 teaspoon Dijon
   mustard
   Salt and fresh pepper
   to taste
¼ cup olive oil or more
2 tablespoons chopped
   flat-leaf parsley

1. Wash and dry the lettuces. Cut or tear into serving pieces and arrange on six chilled plates.
2. Julienne the ham as fine as possible. Melt the butter in a small sauté pan and let it become brown but not burned. Toss the ham in the butter to frizzle it. Cook 2 minutes and add the vinegar. Allow the vinegar to evaporate.
3. Meanwhile, put the chopped egg whites in a small bowl. Add the water, mustard, salt, and pepper and mix. Add enough oil to make the mixture fluid.
4. Sprinkle the ham mixture over each salad and spoon dressing over each. Garnish with the chopped parsley. Serves 6.

Note: When prosciutto is unavailable, use other well-flavored ham.

Gorgonzola Salad Dressing

Serve this dressing over shredded spinach placed in a large balloon-shaped goblet. Or toss it with greens.

2 eggs	Salt and fresh pepper to taste
1 cup oil	½ cup Gorgonzola cheese, cut into pieces
Juice of 1 lemon	
1 garlic clove, chopped	

Place all the ingredients in a food processor or blender. Blend until smooth and creamy. Makes 1½ cups.

Note: Parmesan cheese can be substituted for the Gorgonzola.

Raw Mushroom Salad

2 pounds large white
  mushrooms
Juice of 2 lemons
½ cup olive oil
  Salt and fresh pepper
  to taste

½ teaspoon chopped
  fresh oregano
2 tablespoons chopped
  flat-leaf parsley

1. Clean the mushrooms with a damp cloth. Cut off the
   stems even with the base of the mushrooms. Reserve
   the stems for another use. Slice the caps paper thin.
2. Put the slices in a bowl and add the lemon juice, oil,
   salt, pepper, and oregano. Mix together well and sprinkle parsley over. Serve at room temperature. Serves
   4–6.

Mushroom Salad with Truffles

This is a beautiful salad, but don't make the mistake of
using too much dressing. A few colorful lettuce leaves
around the edge of the salad bowl would be attractive.

2 pounds white
  mushrooms, stems
  removed
  Salt and fresh pepper
  to taste
2 tablespoons chopped
  flat-leaf parsley

2 tablespoons lemon
  juice or red wine
  vinegar
6 tablespoons olive oil
  Few truffle shavings
½ cup Parmesan cheese
  slivers

Clean the mushrooms with a damp cloth and slice as
thin as possible. Place in a serving bowl and add salt,
pepper, parsley, and the lemon juice or vinegar. Pour the
oil over and toss well to mix. Scatter the truffles and
cheese over the top. Serves 4–6.

Tomatoes Filled with Rice Salad

4–6 large ripe tomatoes
   Rice salad (see
   page 29)

4–6 sprigs flat-leaf
   parsley

1. Cut slices off the bottom of the tomatoes, but not completely. They should be able to lift up but be connected with skin, as for a hinge. Cut a tiny hole in center of the lid with the point of a knife. Carefully hollow out the tomatoes and turn upside down to drain.
2. Fill the tomato shells with some of the rice salad. Place lids over rice and stick a piece of parsley through the center of the hinged top for decoration. Set the tomatoes on a platter. Surround with remaining rice salad. Serves 4–6.

Note: A grapefruit knife or melon baller may be helpful for hollowing out tomatoes.

Arturo's Prosciutto Salad

¾ pound prosciutto
2 Golden Delicious
   apples, peeled and
   diced
½ cup slivered almonds,
   blanched and toasted
2 cups celery thinly
   sliced on the diagonal

¼ cup sliced scallions
   Juice of 1 lemon
2–3 tablespoons olive oil
   Salt and fresh
   pepper to taste
⅓ cup mayonnaise
   Salad greens

1. Remove any fat or rind on the ham. Chop the ham and grind in a food processor.
2. Put the ham in a salad bowl and add the apples, almonds, celery, and scallions.
3. Pour on the lemon juice, oil, salt, and pepper. Fold in the mayonnaise. Toss the salad and serve on greens. Serves 4–6.

Orange and Lemon Salad

There is no vinegar in this salad as the acid in the oranges
and lemons is enough. This is also good with just blood
oranges, oil, and lots of pepper.

4 large oranges
1 large lemon
½ cup sliced scallions
¼ cup chopped fresh
   mint
Salt and fresh pepper
to taste

4 tablespoons olive oil
1 head leaf lettuce, torn
   or cut into bite-size
   pieces

1. Peel and section the oranges and lemon and place in
   a salad bowl. Add the scallions, chopped mint, salt,
   and pepper.
2. Pour olive oil over the fruit and mix thoroughly. Add
   chilled lettuce to the salad bowl and toss lightly. Serves
   4–6.

Orange and Garlic Salad

A strange combination that tastes especially good. You
don't need vinegar or lemon juice in this salad—the acid
of the orange accentuated by the garlic does the job just
fine.

6 large oranges, peeled
   and sectioned
6 tablespoons olive oil
2 garlic cloves, chopped
Salt and fresh pepper
to taste

2 tablespoons chopped
   flat-leaf parsley
1 head radicchio

1. Cut each orange section into two pieces. Place in a
   bowl. Add the oil, garlic, salt, pepper, and parsley.
   Mix together gently.

2. Wash and dry the lettuce. Place on six salad plates and spoon the orange mixture over each salad. Serves 4–6.

Macaroni Salad

As American as apple pie, this salad was perhaps the forerunner of the pasta salads so popular in America today. An old-fashioned homey delight.

½ pound cooked elbow
  macaroni
1 medium onion,
  chopped
1 cup diced celery
⅓ cup diced green
  pepper

Salt and fresh pepper
  to taste
1 cup mayonnaise (see
  following recipe)
Salad greens

Place the drained macaroni in a large bowl. Add the onion, celery, green pepper, salt, and pepper. Mix all the ingredients together. Add the mayonnaise and toss together. Serve on salad greens. Serves 4–6.

Basic Mayonnaise

3 egg yolks
  Salt and fresh pepper
  to taste
1 teaspoon Dijon
  mustard

1½ cups oil (any kind
  you prefer)
1–2 tablespoons lemon
  juice

1. In a small bowl, mix the egg yolks, salt, pepper, and mustard. Whisk until sticky. Begin adding the oil, a teaspoonful at a time. Continue to whisk until the mixture thickens.
2. Add the oil, a little more rapidly in a thin stream, as you whisk. Finish with 1–2 tablespoons lemon juice, depending on the consistency desired. Makes 1½ cups.

Pasta Vinaigrette

½ pound cooked penne
  or short macaroni
2 green peppers, seeds
  and filaments
  removed, chopped
4 tomatoes, peeled,
  seeded, and chopped
2 garlic cloves, chopped

1 large onion, chopped
½ cup olive oil
½ cup lemon juice
2 tablespoons chopped
  flat-leaf parsley
Salt and fresh pepper
  to taste

Place the drained hot pasta in a large bowl with the peppers and tomatoes. Add the garlic, onion, oil, and lemon juice. Sprinkle with parsley, salt, and pepper. Toss and serve while still warm. Serves 4–6.

Beefsteak Tomato and Red Onion Salad

5 beefsteak tomatoes
2 red onions
  Salt and fresh pepper
  to taste
¼ cup red wine vinegar

¾ cup olive oil
2 garlic cloves, chopped
2 tablespoons chopped
  flat-leaf parsley

1. Trim off the tops and bottoms of the tomatoes. Cut the tomatoes into ½-inch slices.
2. Peel the onions and cut into ⅛-inch slices. Alternate onions and tomatoes on a long, narrow platter.
3. Whisk together the salt, pepper, vinegar, oil, and garlic. Pour over the tomatoes and onions. Sprinkle the parsley over and serve. Serves 4–6.

Fresh Fig Salad

When figs are in season, this makes a change from the usual salad.

¾ cup chopped
   prosciutto
½ cup thinly sliced
   scallions

6 fresh figs
   Garden lettuce
4 tablespoons olive oil
2 tablespoons vinegar

1. Combine the prosciutto and scallions in a bowl.
2. Cut the figs in half and arrange on fresh garden lettuce. Place a tablespoon of ham mixture on each fig half, or in between fig halves as desired. Spoon the oil and vinegar over each serving. Serves 4–6.

Rice Salad

1 cup long-grain rice
   Salt and fresh pepper
   to taste
¼ cup olive oil
2 tablespoons red wine
   vinegar
½ cup finely diced green
   pepper
½ cup peeled and diced
   cucumbers

2 cups mixed cooked
   vegetables of your
   choice, such as
   carrots, green beans,
   peas
   Lettuce leaves or
   tomatoes

1. Put the rice in a heavy 1½-quart pan or casserole. Add 2 cups water. Bring to a boil, turn to a simmer, put on lid, and cook 20 minutes.
2. When cooked, transfer the rice to a bowl. Fluff up with two forks. Add the salt, pepper, oil, vinegar, and vegetables and toss well to mix.
3. Serve on lettuce leaves, pack into a ring mold and invert onto a platter, or use to fill tomatoes. Serves 4–6.

Variation

Omit the vegetables and add ¼ cup drained capers to the rice with the oil and vinegar.

Radicchio and Fennel Salad

Radicchio comes in two shapes: a long narrow head from Treviso and a solid round head from Castlefranco.

½ cup pitted and
chopped black olives
4 tablespoons white
wine vinegar
2 anchovy fillets,
drained, rinsed, and
chopped, or salt-
packed anchovies

Fresh pepper to taste
½ cup olive oil
2 large fennel bulbs
1 large head radicchio
or 2 small ones

1. Place half the olives in a bowl with the vinegar, anchovies, and pepper. Mix together. Add the oil and blend.
2. Discard the fennel stalks and root ends. Cut the fennel into julienne strips. Place in a salad bowl.
3. Separate the radicchio leaves and tear or cut into bite-size pieces. Mix with the fennel.
4. Pour the dressing over, add the rest of the olives, and toss gently to mix well. Serves 4–6.

Green Bean and Salami Salad

2 medium potatoes,
peeled and diced
1 pound green beans,
trimmed
½ cup olive oil
¼ cup red wine vinegar
1 garlic clove, chopped

2 scallions, sliced
Salt and fresh pepper
to taste
6 slices hard salami, cut
into thin strips
2 tablespoons chopped
flat-leaf parsley

1. Cook the diced potato in water to cover until tender, 5–7 minutes. Drain and place in a bowl.
2. Bring a kettle of salted water to a boil and drop in the beans. Cook uncovered until barely tender, 5–7 minutes, depending upon the age of the beans. Drain the beans and plunge into ice water to refresh. Drain and dry them. Add to the potatoes.

3. Combine the oil, vinegar, garlic, scallions, salt, and pepper. Pour over the potatoes and beans. Place the salami and parsley on top and toss gently. Serves 6.

Summer Squash Salad

¼ cup wine vinegar
6 tablespoons olive oil
1 garlic clove, chopped
2 teaspoons Dijon
   mustard
   Salt and fresh pepper
   to taste
½ pound cooked
   mostaccioli, or other
   tubular pasta

1 cup coarsely chopped
   peeled tomato
¾ cup thinly sliced
   yellow squash
¾ cup thinly sliced
   zucchini
1 cucumber, peeled,
   seeded, and chopped

Whisk together the vinegar, oil, garlic, mustard, salt, and pepper. In a large bowl, combine the remaining ingredients. Pour the dressing over the pasta mixture. Toss lightly until evenly coated. Serves 4–6.

Garden Salad Pasta

½ cup olive oil
   Juice of 2 lemons
1 garlic clove, chopped
   Salt and fresh pepper
   to taste
1 teaspoon marjoram or
   oregano
2 medium tomatoes,
   peeled and cut into
   wedges
1 medium cucumber,
   peeled and thinly
   sliced

1 medium green
   pepper, cut into
   strips
6 radishes, thinly sliced
4 scallions, sliced
12 pitted ripe olives
2 tablespoons chopped
   flat-leaf parsley
½ pound cooked shell
   pasta

Combine the oil, lemon juice, garlic, salt, pepper, and marjoram in a small bowl. Beat with a wire whisk until blended. Combine the remaining ingredients in a large bowl. Just before serving, toss with dressing to coat the pasta mixture. Serves 4–6.

Pepperoni Salad

6 tablespoons olive oil
4 tablespoons wine
  vinegar
4 basil leaves, chopped
  Salt and fresh pepper
  to taste
2 cups cooked Italian
  green beans

¼ pound pepperoni,
  thinly sliced and cut
  into quarters
½ pound cooked snail-
  shaped pasta

Whisk the oil, vinegar, basil, salt, and pepper until blended. Combine the remaining ingredients in a large bowl. Stir in dressing; toss to coat the pasta mixture. Serves 4–6.

Chicken and Pasta Salad

½ cup olive oil
4 tablespoons red
  wine vinegar
2 teaspoons Dijon
  mustard
  Salt and fresh
  pepper to taste
1½ cups cubed cooked
  chicken
¼ cup chopped pitted
  black olives

¼ cup chopped red
  pepper
¼ cup chopped dill
  pickle
½ pound cooked shell
  pasta
¾ cup cubed Swiss
  cheese

Whisk together the oil, vinegar, mustard, salt, and pepper. Combine the remaining ingredients in a large bowl. Pour the dressing over the pasta mixture. Toss lightly until evenly coated. Serves 4–6.

Lemon Pasta Salad

½ pound cooked
  linguine
8 tablespoons olive oil
  Juice of 2 large
  lemons
  Salt and fresh pepper
  to taste

1 tablespoon chopped
  flat-leaf parsley
½ cup chopped fresh
  basil leaves
1 garlic clove, finely
  chopped

Place the cooked pasta in a large bowl. Add the oil and mix well. Squeeze on the lemon juice and sprinkle with salt and pepper. Add the parsley, basil, and garlic and toss. Serve warm or at room temperature. Serves 4–6.

Primavera Salad

½ cup olive oil
¼ cup white wine
  vinegar
1 teaspoon Dijon
  mustard
1 garlic clove, chopped
  Salt and fresh pepper
  to taste
½ pound cooked pasta
  twists
2 cups cooked fresh
  asparagus cut into
  1-inch pieces

2 cups thinly sliced
  zucchini
2 cups sliced fresh
  mushrooms
1 red pepper, cut into
  strips
½ cup sliced scallions
2 tablespoons chopped
  flat-leaf parsley

Whisk the oil, vinegar, mustard, garlic, salt, and pepper until well blended. Combine the remaining ingredients in a large bowl. Pour the dressing over the pasta mixture. Toss lightly until evenly coated. Serves 6.

Pasta and Green Bean Salad

1 pound green beans,
  cut into 1-inch pieces
½ pound cooked fusilli
½ cup olive oil
2 tablespoons red wine
  vinegar
1 teaspoon chopped
  oregano

1 garlic clove,
  chopped
Salt and fresh
  pepper to taste
3–4 basil leaves,
  chopped

1. Add the green beans to boiling salted water. Cook, uncovered, 5 minutes. Drain and refresh in cold water. Dry the beans.
2. Combine the beans and the cooked pasta in a large bowl. Add the oil, vinegar, oregano, garlic, salt, and pepper. Toss well to blend. Garnish with chopped basil leaves. Serves 4–6.

Pasta and Shredded Carrot Salad

½ pound cooked
  spaghettini
1 cup shredded carrots
2 tablespoons red wine
  vinegar
½ cup olive oil
2 tablespoons chopped
  flat-leaf parsley

2 tablespoons
  chopped scallions
3–4 basil leaves,
  chopped
Salt and fresh
  pepper to taste

Combine the cooked pasta and shredded carrots in a large bowl. Add the vinegar, oil, parsley, scallions, and basil and toss gently to mix. Season with salt and pepper and toss again. Serves 4–6.

3

VEGETABLES

WHO NEEDS MEAT WHEN YOU HAVE EGGPLANT? Eggplant Parmesan, eggplant fried and made into a crispy cheese sandwich, eggplant simply split lengthwise, brushed with olive oil, and run under the broiler. Italians have come up with more recipes for this versatile vegetable than any other people, I believe. And with almost as many more recipes for zucchini.

Most of the recipes in this section are entrees in themselves. The exceptions are the leafy greens, sautéed in olive oil and garlic (and served with a wedge of lemon, of course). Italians believe that eating greens every day guarantees a long life. I don't know about that—but greens are so quick and easy to cook that it seems as if you have a lot more time to fix dinner when you make them.

I have not included spaghetti squash in this section— a fad that has started to fade, but still a good low-calorie, if expensive, substitute for pasta. I remember when I took a few spaghetti squash to Italy, the chefs were amazed when I pulled those long strips of squash apart and served them with tomato sauce. To me, spaghetti squash seems to taste best when you're amazing someone. And most people are no longer amazed.

Vegetable Lasagne

1 medium eggplant	1 teaspoon oregano or
5–6 tablespoons olive oil	thyme
1½ pounds spinach	4 eggs
3 tablespoons butter	½ cup freshly grated
Salt and fresh	Parmesan cheese
pepper	1½ cups tomato sauce
1 pound ricotta	I. (see page 102)
cheese	
½ pound mozzarella	
cheese, grated	

1. Peel the eggplant and cut it lengthwise into ¼-inch slices.
2. In a large sauté pan, heat 5–6 tablespoons olive oil. When very hot, sauté the eggplant to brown on both sides. Drain the slices on paper towels as they are cooked.
3. Wash the spinach and trim off the heavy stems. Heat the butter in a large sauté pan, and add the spinach. Cook 3–4 minutes until spinach is wilted. Add salt and pepper.
4. Allow to cool, then place in a towel and squeeze out most of the liquid. Chop the spinach roughly.
5. Put the ricotta, mozzarella, and oregano in a bowl. Add the eggs and mix well. Add the prepared spinach and mix well.
6. Oil a rectangular low-sided baking dish. Lay in one layer of eggplant, then a layer of the spinach mixture, a layer of eggplant, a layer of spinach, a layer of eggplant. Finish with the spinach mixture. Sprinkle

with Parmesan cheese. Bake at 375 degrees for 30–40 minutes until bubbly. Serve with tomato sauce. Serves 4–6.

Stuffed Artichokes

6 artichokes
12 tablespoons butter
2½ cups chopped onion
1 cup bread crumbs
½ cup freshly grated Parmesan cheese

Salt and pepper to taste
Olive oil to film baking dish

1. Break off the stems and trim the bases of the artichokes so they will stand. Trim the tips of the leaves with scissors. Cut off ½ inch from the top of each artichoke.
2. Put into a large kettle of boiling water and cook uncovered for 25–35 minutes, or until done. Drain upside down on a towel.
3. Remove the center cones from each artichoke and scrape out the hairy choke.
4. Melt 2 tablespoons of the butter in a medium skillet and add the chopped onion. Sauté 5 minutes until wilted. Remove to a bowl and add the bread crumbs, cheese, salt, and pepper.
5. Melt the remainder of the butter and add some of it to the onion-cheese mixture. Add just enough to moisten. Stuff into the artichokes.
6. Film an ovenproof dish with olive oil and arrange artichokes in the dish. Drizzle any remaining butter over the artichokes. Bake at 400 degrees for 15 minutes. Serve warm or at room temperature. Serves 6.

Basil Custards

1 tablespoon butter
2 tablespoons chopped
  onion
1/4 cup coarsely chopped
  basil leaves
2 eggs

2 egg yolks
1½ cups cream
Salt and fresh
pepper to taste
Butter for greasing
molds

1. Melt the butter in very small skillet. Add the onion and cook 2–3 minutes to soften.
2. Place in a blender jar the basil, eggs, egg yolks, and cream. Blend until smooth.
3. Add the onion, salt, and pepper. Blend until well mixed.
4. Grease six custard cups. Fill each cup two-thirds full. Set the molds in a water bath, allowing the water to come halfway up the sides of the molds. Bake at 350 degrees for 20–25 minutes, or just until set. Let stand a few minutes, unmold, and serve. Serves 6.

Sautéed Dandelion Greens

6 tablespoons olive oil
2 garlic cloves, chopped
3 pounds dandelion
  greens, washed and
  roots trimmed

Salt and fresh pepper to
taste
Lemon wedges

1. Heat the olive oil in a large stockpot. When hot, add the garlic and stir for 1 minute. Do not brown.
2. Add the prepared greens with the water clinging to them, season with salt and pepper and cook, while stirring with a wooden spatula, until greens are wilted. Serve with lemon wedges. Serves 4–6.

Italian Green Beans

1–1½ pounds Italian
green beans, cut
into 1-inch pieces
½ cup chopped onion
½ cup chopped
celery
1 garlic clove,
chopped
4–5 basil leaves,
chopped

1 tablespoon chopped
fresh rosemary
Salt and fresh
pepper to taste
1 tablespoon olive oil
Toasted pine nuts
for garnish (see
note)

1. Place the beans in a saucepan and add the onion, celery, garlic, basil, and rosemary. Add just enough boiling water to barely cover.
2. Bring to a boil and cook, uncovered, until the beans are tender crisp, 5–10 minutes.
3. Drain. Do not refresh. Add salt, pepper, and olive oil. Garnish with pine nuts sprinkled over the top. Serves 4–6.

Note: To toast pine nuts, lay them on a baking sheet. Bake 10 minutes at 350 degrees.

Broccoli with Ripe Olives

3 pounds broccoli,
coarse stem ends and
leaves removed
½ cup olive oil
2 garlic cloves, mashed
¾ cup chopped ripe
olives

½ cup dry white wine
Juice of 1 lemon
Salt and fresh pepper
to taste

1. Separate the broccoli into stalks. Cut an X in the base of the stems to allow them to cook as quickly as the heads. In a shallow saucepan or skillet, bring 2 inches of water to a boil. Add the broccoli. Cover the pan tightly and cook 10–12 minutes, or until broccoli is just tender. Drain. Refresh in cold water. Dry on towels.

2. Heat the oil in a skillet. Add the garlic and cook for 1–2 minutes. Remove the garlic.

3. Add the olives, white wine, and lemon juice. Add the broccoli and cook 1–2 minutes, turning broccoli carefully so it is well coated with the oil and olive mixture. Season with salt and pepper. Turn out into a serving dish. Serves 4–6.

Baked Broccoli Stems

Here is a chance to use up the stems from broccoli.

2 cups ricotta cheese
1 cup finely chopped
  cooked broccoli stems
½ cup grated Parmesan
  cheese
¼ cup flour

2 eggs, slightly beaten
Salt and fresh pepper
to taste
Touch of grated
nutmeg

1. In a large bowl, combine the ricotta cheese, broccoli, ¼ cup of the Parmesan cheese, flour, eggs, salt, pepper, and nutmeg.

2. Spoon into a 9-inch shallow pie dish. Sprinkle with the remaining cheese. Bake 30 minutes at 350˚ degrees, or until the top is lightly browned. Serves 6–8.

Cauliflower with Anchovy Butter

*1 medium to large head
 cauliflower
1 teaspoon salt*

*Anchovy butter (see
 following recipe)*

1. Remove the leaves and tough stems from the cauliflower. Divide into flowerets.
2. In a large pot, bring enough water to a boil to just accommodate the cauliflower. Add salt. Add the cauliflower, cover, and boil gently 8–12 minutes until cauliflower is just tender. Drain.
3. Spoon the anchovy butter over. Serves 4–6.

Anchovy Butter

Serve over cauliflower or broccoli or spoon over broiled fish. Use as a dip for raw vegetables or spoon over toast to serve with drinks.

*8 tablespoons butter,
 softened
4 anchovy fillets,
 drained, rinsed, and
 dried*

*1 tablespoon chopped
 flat-leaf parsley*

Work butter, anchovies, and parsley to a paste in a mortar and pestle, or cream together in a food processor. Melt and serve. Makes ½ cup.

Variation

Melt the butter in a small pan, add anchovies and cook till they dissolve, add parsley and use as above.

Cauliflower or Broccoli with Prosciutto

2 tablespoons olive oil
1 garlic clove, chopped
⅛ pound prosciutto,
  chopped
  Cauliflower or
  broccoli, separated
  into flowerets and
  cooked according to
  recipe on page 43.

Salt and fresh pepper
  to taste
2 tablespoons freshly
  grated Parmesan
  cheese

Heat the oil in a skillet. Add the garlic and sauté 1 minute. Add the prosciutto and cook another minute. Sprinkle over the vegetable and season with salt and pepper. Sprinkle with cheese. Serves 4–6.

Eggplant Boats

To turn this into a main dish, a little ground meat could be sautéed and added to the filling.

4 small eggplants
  Salt
  Juice of 1 lemon
6 tablespoons olive oil
2 tablespoons butter
1 onion, chopped
4 tomatoes, peeled,
  seeded, and roughly
  chopped
2 garlic cloves,
  chopped
1–2 tablespoons
  chopped flat-leaf
  parsley

2 bay leaves, crushed
½ teaspoon thyme
  Fresh pepper to
  taste
¼ cup fresh bread
  crumbs
2 small tomatoes,
  thinly sliced
  (optional)
2 tablespoons butter

1. Cut the eggplants in half lengthwise. Cut a line all round the eggplants ¼ inch from the edge, then slash the flesh. Sprinkle with salt and lemon juice.
2. In a large sauté pan, heat the olive oil. When very hot, add the eggplant cut side down and cook until browned.
3. Transfer to a baking sheet. Place in a 350-degree oven and bake 10–15 minutes until flesh is just soft.
4. Allow to cool a bit, then scoop out the flesh leaving a ⅛-inch shell. Chop the flesh roughly. Set the shells aside.
5. Melt 2 tablespoons of butter in a large sauté pan and add the onion. Cook to wilt. Add the chopped eggplant, chopped tomatoes, garlic, parsley, bay leaves, thyme, salt, and pepper. Stir in the bread crumbs to tighten the mixture slightly. Pack loosely into the shells.
6. Place the filled shells in an oiled baking dish. Top the eggplants with 2–3 slices tomato. Add bits of butter to each. Bake at 360 degreees for 15–20 minutes, until lightly browned. Serves 8.

Sautéed Eggplant Parmesan

In America, eggplant is almost always fried. In Italy, it is fried and baked and broiled, and made into what is certainly one of the world's greatest vegetarian dishes—eggplant Parmesan.

*1 large eggplant, cut
  into ½-to 1-inch slices*
½ cup flour
1 cup bread crumbs
*¼ cup freshly grated
  Parmesan cheese*
2 eggs

½ cup heavy cream
6 tablespoons olive oil
*Salt and fresh pepper
  to taste*
*2 tablespoons chopped
  flat-leaf parsley*

1. Peel the eggplant, if desired.
2. Place the flour in a shallow plate. Combine the bread crumbs and cheese and place in another shallow plate.
3. Beat the eggs and cream together in a shallow bowl.
4. Dip the eggplant slices into flour, then the egg mixture, and finally in the bread crumb mixture.
5. Heat the oil in a large skillet. When hot, sauté a few pieces at a time until brown on both sides, 1–2 minutes on each side. Season with salt, pepper, and parsley. Keep warm in a 200-degree oven while sautéeing the remainder. Serves 4–6.

Variation

Sautéed eggplant, as above

2 cups tomato sauce I or II (see pages 102–103)

1 cup freshly grated Parmesan cheese

1 cup diced mozzarella cheese

Few basil leaves

Baked eggplant parmesan. Spoon a thin layer of tomato sauce into the bottom of an 8- by 10-inch baking dish. Next, place a layer of the sautéed eggplant. Sprinkle with Parmesan cheese and a few pieces of mozzarella cheese. Alternate layers until all the eggplant is used. Place basil leaves in the middle. End with a layer of tomato sauce and remaining cheese. Bake at 350 degrees for 25 minutes, or until bubbling and hot. Serves 4–6.

Eggplant Sandwiches

It is easiest to slice the eggplant if you use a mandoline. The sandwiches or rolls can also be cut into small pieces to serve with drinks.

½ cup flour
2 eggs
½ cup heavy cream
1 cup bread crumbs
¼ cup freshly grated
    Parmesan cheese
2 medium eggplants,
    sliced lengthwise into
    ¼-inch slices

6 tablespoons olive oil
Mozzarella cheese,
    diced
Anchovy fillets,
    drained
Oregano

1. Put the flour in a shallow plate.
2. Beat the eggs with the cream in a shallow bowl.
3. Combine the bread crumbs and cheese on another shallow plate.
4. Dip the eggplant in flour, then eggs, then bread crumb mixture and sauté in oil 1–2 minutes a side.
5. Lay the sautéed eggplant on a baking sheet. On half the slices, place a spoonful of mozzarella cheese, an anchovy, and a pinch of oregano. Lay a slice of eggplant on top, as for sandwiches.
6. Bake in a 375-degree oven for 10–15 minutes, or until the cheese melts. Serve plain or with tomato sauce. Serves 4–6.

Variation

Eggplant rolls. Instead of making sandwiches, the eggplant can be rolled. Do not put a slice of eggplant on top of the other. Simply roll the slice of sautéed eggplant containing the cheese, oregano, and anchovy. Fasten with a toothpick and bake at 375 degrees for 10–15 minutes. Serve plain or with tomato sauce. Or place a thin layer of tomato sauce in the bottom of the baking dish. Lay the rolls on the sauce. Cover with more sauce and bake at 375 degrees for 10–15 minutes.

Stuffed Eggplant

3 medium eggplants
6 strips bacon, cut up
1 cup chopped onion
1 cup chopped green
  peppers
4 tomatoes, peeled,
  seeded, and chopped

4 basil leaves, chopped
  Salt and fresh pepper
  to taste
1 cup buttered bread
  crumbs
½ cup freshly grated
  Parmesan cheese

1. Cut the eggplants in half lengthwise. Scrape out the pulp leaving a ½-inch shell. Blanch the shells in boiling water a few minutes; invert on paper towels to drain. Chop the pulp and set aside.
2. Preheat the oven to 350 degrees.
3. In a large skillet, cook the bacon just until it begins to brown. Add the chopped eggplant and remaining ingredients except bread crumbs and cheese. Cook, stirring, until the eggplant is tender, about 5 minutes.
4. Spoon the mixture into the eggplant shells. Arrange the shells in a shallow baking dish. Top the eggplant mixture with crumbs and cheese. Bake 15–20 minutes until hot. Makes 4–6 servings.

Variation

Peel the eggplant and dice the pulp. Preheat the oven and proceed as above. Spoon the mixture into a 1-quart baking dish. Top with crumbs and cheese. Bake 15–20 minutes.

Jean's Eggplant

1 medium eggplant,
  cubed
1 egg, slightly beaten
6 medium tomatoes,
  peeled, seeded, and
  chopped
4 tablespoons butter,
  melted
1 onion, chopped

½ cup dry bread crumbs
  Salt and fresh pepper
  to taste
½ cup buttered fresh
  bread crumbs (see
  note)
½ cup freshly grated
  Parmesan cheese

1. Cook the eggplant in boiling water to cover for 5 minutes. Drain.
2. Place in a bowl and add the egg, tomatoes, butter, onion, dry crumbs, salt, and pepper. Mix well to combine.
3. Place in a buttered 8-inch baking dish. Top with buttered crumbs. Sprinkle with cheese. Bake at 350 degrees for 30 minutes. Serves 4–6.

Note: To make buttered crumbs, melt 2 tablespoons butter in a small pan. Tear 2 slices of bread, without crusts, into little pieces. Toss the bread with the butter.

Celery with Toasted Pine Nuts

This also works well with fennel.

1 large bunch celery
  (enough to make 4
  cups sliced)
4 tablespoons butter
1 small onion, chopped
  Salt and fresh pepper
  to taste

½ cup toasted pine nuts
  (see note)
1 tablespoon chopped
  flat-leaf parsley

1. Wash the celery. Cut the ribs into diagonal pieces 1 inch long.
2. Melt the butter in a saucepan and add the onion and celery. Cover and cook, shaking the pan, until the celery is tender crisp, about 15 minutes.
3. Remove the lid. Stir in the salt, pepper, pine nuts, and parsley and serve. Serves 4–6.

Note: To toast pine nuts, lay them on a baking sheet. Bake 10 minutes at 350 degrees.

Escarole

Escarole is a forgotten green, for no good reason I can think of. It's a good addition to salads, and excellent served as a vegetable sautéed in olive oil and garlic. Better yet, sauté escarole and then toss it with pasta—it makes a low-cost, low-calorie, and excellent entree.

*1½–2 pounds escarole
6 tablespoons butter
2 garlic cloves, mashed*

*Salt and fresh pepper
to taste*

1. Wash the escarole and remove the leaves. Place the leaves in a saucepan. Cover with boiling water and cook 5 minutes, or until leaves are tender. Drain the leaves and dry them on toweling.
2. Heat the butter in a large skillet and add the garlic. Stir the garlic in the butter for 2–3 minutes; discard garlic.
3. Add the escarole and stir around until well coated with butter. Add salt and pepper. Serves 4–6.

Fennel with Parmesan Cheese

This is one vegetable I prefer almost overcooked.

4–5 bulbs fennel
  8 tablespoons butter
    or more, melted
¾ cup freshly grated
    Parmesan cheese

Salt and fresh pepper
to taste

1. Trim the fennel by removing the base and cutting off
   the feathery tops. Reserve enough of the feathery tops
   to chop to make ¼ cup. Remove the coarse outside
   layer of each bulb. Cut the fennel into julienne strips.
2. Place the fennel in a saucepan and cover with water.
   Bring to a boil, covered. Reduce to moderate heat and
   cook fennel 10–15 minutes, or until tender. Drain and
   place in a baking dish.
3. Sprinkle with the melted butter, cheese, chopped fennel tops, salt, and pepper. Mix to combine. Bake at
   375 degrees for 20 minutes, or until very soft. Serves
   4–6.

Variation

2 pounds celery, trimmed
  and cut into thin slices

1 tablespoon anisette

Celery with Parmesan. Prepare the recipe as above,
substituting celery for fennel. Drizzle the anisette over
just before baking.

To be thoroughly Italian, you should probably make
this with Sambuca instead of anisette. But anisette is
cheaper and you will never notice the difference on celery.
The way to serve Sambuca as a liqueur is "con mosche"—
with three coffee beans floating on top so they look like
fat dead flies. There's a tradition in Italy that if you don't
get mosche in your Sambuca it means the restaurant does

not want you to come back, and wishes you bad luck
besides. So if you don't get your mosche, leave quickly
before something worse happens.

Mushrooms with Marsala

4 tablespoons butter
¼ cup chopped onion
1½ pounds mushrooms,
  cleaned and sliced
¼ cup Marsala
¾ cup heavy cream

Salt and freshly
cracked white pepper
to taste
1 tablespoon chopped
flat-leaf parsley

1. Heat the butter in a large skillet. Add the onion and
   cook, stirring with a wooden spatula, for 3 minutes.
2. Add the mushrooms and toss or stir for 3 minutes
   longer.
3. Add the Marsala and cook until all the juices in the
   pan are evaporated. (This intensifies the flavor.)
4. Add the cream and continue to cook until it coats a
   spoon. Season with salt and pepper and garnish with
   parsley. Serves 4–6.

Stuffed Mushrooms

1 pound large
  mushrooms
¼ cup fresh bread
  crumbs
1 tablespoon chopped
  scallions
Salt and fresh
pepper to taste

1–2 tablespoons dry
  Marsala
¼ cup chopped
  prosciutto
1 tablespoon olive oil

1. Clean the mushrooms with a damp cloth. Remove and
   chop the stems and place in a bowl.

2. Add the bread crumbs, scallions, salt, pepper, and wine
   to moisten. Add the prosciutto and mix well. Pack into
   the mushroom caps.
3. Place the mushrooms on a baking sheet and drizzle the
   olive oil over. Bake at 350 degrees for 15 minutes, or
   until the stuffing is brown. Serves 4–6.

Note: For a cheese flavor, sprinkle a little freshly grated
Parmesan cheese over the stuffed mushrooms.

Peas with Ham

4 tablespoons butter
1 small onion,
  chopped
2½ pounds peas, shelled
1½ cups chicken stock

¼ pound prosciutto,
  diced
Fresh pepper to
taste

1. Heat the butter in a saucepan. Add the onion and stir
   around in the butter for 2–3 minutes.
2. Add the peas and chicken stock. Cover and bring to
   a boil. Turn to a simmer and cook 10 minutes, or until
   peas are tender.
3. Add the prosciutto and toss with the peas over medium
   heat until heated through. Season with pepper. Serves
   4–6.

Note: Chicken stock may be drained from the peas, placed
in a small pan, and reduced to 2 or 3 tablespoons. Return
to the peas.

Stewed Sliced Peppers

Double this recipe and keep some aside for a sauce for
pasta.

¼ cup olive oil, or
   enough to film the
   bottom of a medium
   saucepan
1 large onion, sliced
   thin
6–8 red and yellow
   peppers, or green
   and red, seeds
   removed and thinly
   sliced

1–2 mint leaves,
   chopped
Few sprigs oregano,
   chopped
Salt and fresh
   pepper to taste

1. Heat the olive oil in a saucepan. Add the onion and
   cook over a medium flame until wilted, 3–4 minutes.
2. Add the peppers, mint, and oregano. Stir with a wooden
   spatula to mix. Turn the heat to low. Cover and cook,
   stirring occasionally, for 25–30 minutes. If the peppers
   get dry, add a bit of water. Season with salt and pepper.
   Serve warm. Serves 4–6.

Variation

Omit the mint and add 1 garlic clove, chopped, along
with the onion.

Roasted Onions

These onions are delicious served plain or with oil and
vinegar.

1 large onion per person
   Salt and fresh pepper
   to taste

Cruets of olive oil and
   red wine vinegar

1. Place whole unpeeled and unwashed onions on a baking sheet. Bake in a 500-degree oven for 10 minutes.

2. Reduce the oven temperatures to 400 degrees and bake 40–45 minutes. Pierce with the point of a small knife to test if tender.
3. To serve, split open the onion and season with salt and pepper, oil, and vinegar. Serves 1 per person.

Onions Steamed in Chianti

Serve this to onion haters; they will love it.

6 tablespoons butter
8 medium-large onions, peeled and sliced
¼ cup sugar
½ cup red wine vinegar

1 cup Chianti
Salt and fresh pepper to taste
¼ cup freshly grated Parmesan cheese

1. Melt the butter in a large sauté pan. Add the sliced onions. Stir onions in the butter for 15 minutes, using a wooden spatula.
2. Add the sugar, vinegar, and wine and cook 10 minutes while stirring.
3. Cover, lower the flame, and cook 5 minutes. Remove the lid and season with salt and pepper. Cook over medium heat until the liquid evaporates.
4. Serve plain as a vegetable, either hot or tepid. Or place in a baking dish and sprinkle with freshly grated Parmesan cheese. Bake at 400 degrees for 5 minutes. Or place under a hot broiler for 1 minute. Serves 6.

Onions with Espresso Coffee

4 tablespoons butter
4 large onions, sliced
2 teaspoons sugar
¾ cup espresso coffee

½ cup chicken stock
Salt and fresh pepper to taste

1. Heat the butter in a skillet. Add the onions and cook, stirring, for 15 minutes.
2. Add the sugar and cook 1 minute.
3. Add the coffee, chicken stock, salt, and pepper. Continue to cook and stir occasionally until the liquid reduces and evaporates, 15–20 minutes longer. Serves 4–6.

Fried Peppers

8 large peppers, red, green, yellow, or a combination
¼ cup olive oil

1–2 garlic cloves, chopped
Salt and fresh pepper to taste

1. Cut the peppers in half lengthwise. Remove the seeds and filament. Cut each into strips or squares.
2. Heat the oil in a large skillet. When hot, add the garlic and stir for 1 minute.
3. Add the peppers, salt, and pepper. Cook, stirring with a wooden spatula, for 5–10 minutes, until peppers are tender crisp. Serves 4–6.

Roasted Peppers

I find it simpler to char my peppers under the broiler. But if you want to keep the pepper odor out of the house, char them over the barbecue. Spear them with a fork and grill them over the flame.

Each August a friend supplies me with a bushel basket of gorgeous red peppers. I place them on a baking sheet, leaving a space in between each one. Then I put them under the broiler, 2 inches from the unit. When one side is charred black, I turn them over, using a long pair of tongs. The pepper aroma wafts through the house and lingers for a few days. When the peppers are charred on all sides, I remove the baking sheet from the oven and cover the peppers with a tent of aluminum foil. They will steam. When cool enough to handle, I remove them, one by one, and, holding them over a bowl, I slip off the skin, remove the stem and inside filament along with the seeds. The juice runs into the bowl along with some of the seeds. They can be strained out later. It is better not to lose the precious juice. I cut each pepper into 4 pieces. Place them in a bowl. Strain out seeds from accumulated juice. Cover the peppers with olive oil, perhaps a bit of red wine vinegar, and chopped garlic to taste. Season with salt and pepper to taste. I keep these in the refrigerator, covered, and use them as is or serve them with anchovies. I also put them in small cartons and freeze them.

Baked Roasted Peppers

8 large peppers, red,
  green, or yellow,
  roasted according to
  previous instructions
2 tablespoons capers,
  rinsed and dried
8 anchovies, chopped

½ cup black olives,
  pitted and chopped
Salt and fresh pepper
  to taste
¼ cup dry bread crumbs
½ cup olive oil

1. Place the roasted peppers in a medium-size baking dish. Scatter the capers, anchovies, olives, salt, and pepper over them. Mix them around with a spatula.
2. Sprinkle the surface with bread crumbs and drizzle olive oil over all. Bake at 375 degrees for 10–15 minutes. Serve hot or cold. Serves 4–6.

Potatoes with Peppers

4 tablespoons oil
1 medium onion,
    chopped
1 cup chopped scallion
    tops
1 green pepper, seeds
    and fibers removed,
    chopped
1 red pepper, seeds and
    fibers removed,
    chopped

6 medium potatoes,
    boiled, peeled, and
    thickly sliced
Few sprigs fresh
    rosemary, chopped
Salt and fresh pepper
    to taste

1. Heat the oil in a skillet. When hot, add the onion, scallions, and peppers. Cook, while stirring around with a wooden spatula, for 3 minutes.
2. Add the potatoes and stir to combine. Add the rosemary, salt, and pepper. Toss over a moderate heat until well blended. Serves 4–6.

Adday's Potato Pie

THE CRUST:

¼ cup solid shortening
2 tablespoons oil
2 cups flour

1 teaspoon salt
6 tablespoons warm
    water

THE FILLING:

6 tablespoons butter
½ cup cream
6 medium potatoes,
    peeled, cooked, and
    mashed
    Salt and fresh
    pepper to taste
    Freshly grated
    nutmeg to taste

8 tablespoons butter
1 large onion,
    chopped
1 egg, beaten
1½ cups freshly grated
    Parmesan cheese

1. Cut the shortening and oil into the flour and salt with a pastry blender. Add warm water, a little at a time. Toss with a fork until all the dough comes together to form a ball.
2. Roll out on a lightly floured board into a 13- by 17-inch rectangle. Carefully lay this dough into a pan slightly smaller than the dough, 9 by 13 inches. The dough will extend over the edges of the pan. Set aside.
3. Add the 6 tablespoons butter and cream to the mashed potatoes. Season with salt, pepper, and nutmeg. Beat well.
4. Melt 8 tablespoons butter in a skillet. Add the onion and cook 3–4 minutes.
5. Spread the potatoes over the pastry in the baking pan to within ½ inch of the edge. Scatter the cooked onions over the potatoes. Fold excess pastry back to form a rim inside the edges of the pan.
6. Brush the surface of the potatoes and the pastry with beaten egg. Sprinkle with Parmesan cheese. Bake at 375 degrees for 1 hour. Cut into squares to serve. Serves 6–10.

Parmesan Potatoes

4 large potatoes, peeled and cut into ½-inch slices	Salt and fresh pepper to taste
1 cup freshly grated Parmesan cheese	2 teaspoons chopped rosemary
¼ cup flour	6 slices mozzarella cheese, cut into sticks
8 tablespoons butter, melted	2 inches long and ¼ inch wide (optional)

1. Put the potatoes in a saucepan and cover with water. Bring to a boil, cover, and cook 15 minutes. Drain.
2. Mix the Parmesan cheese and flour together. Roll the potatoes in the cheese mixture on all sides.

3. Pour the melted butter into a baking dish. Lay the coated potatoes over butter in a single layer. Season with salt and pepper and sprinkle with the rosemary. Place in a 350-degree oven for ½ hour, or until tender and brown. Turn once or twice. Cook longer, if necessary.
4. If desired, place pieces of mozzarella cheese around the potatoes 5 minutes before the potatoes are cooked. Serve when the cheese is melted. Serves 6.

Potato Croquettes

These croquettes are just like the American kind, except that they have a delicious little bit of ham and cheese inside. Make them as finger food or larger to serve with an entree.

1 pound potatoes
1 tablespoon butter
Salt and fresh pepper to taste
Freshly grated nutmeg to taste
2 eggs
1 egg yolk

Flour
½ pound mozzarella cheese, cut into ½-inch cubes
½ pound cooked ham, cut into ½-inch cubes
1 cup fine dry bread crumbs

1. Peel the potatoes and cook with water to cover until soft but not mushy; drain. Dry thoroughly by shaking the pan over heat until all the moisture evaporates.
2. Force the potatoes through a ricer or sieve placed over a medium-size bowl. Add butter, salt, pepper, nutmeg, 1 egg, and the egg yolk. Beat until light and fluffy.
3. Using floured hands, shape the potato around the cheese or ham to form small balls. Roll in flour to coat, then in beaten egg, then bread crumbs.
4. Fry in hot fat (375 degrees) a few minutes, or until golden brown. Drain on paper towels. Makes 36.

Grilled Radicchio

6 long heads radicchio   Lemon wedges
12 tablespoons olive oil
Salt and fresh pepper to
taste

1. Wash and dry the radicchio. Cut each head in half lengthwise. Insert a long metal skewer in the root end. Drizzle olive oil over each half.
2. Place over the barbecue and grill 2–3 minutes on each side. Season with salt and pepper. Serve with lemon wedges. Serves 4–6.

Note: To broil, lay the radicchio halves on a broiler rack, cut side up. Drizzle each with half the olive oil. Turn over and drizzle the other side. Place 3–4 inches from the broiler unit. Broil 3 minutes on each side.

Stuffed Yellow Squash

4 medium-size yellow
     squash
2 tablespoons butter
1 pound spinach,
     washed and stems
     removed
½ cup freshly grated
     Parmesan cheese
1 egg
½ teaspoon chopped
     fresh oregano

1 garlic clove, chopped
1 tablespoon chopped
     flat-leaf parsley
     Salt and fresh pepper
     to taste
     Butter for baking dish
¼ cup freshly grated
     Parmesan cheese
¼ cup dry bread crumbs
2 tablespoons olive oil

1. Slice the squash in half lengthwise. Remove the pulp with a spoon. Chop squash pulp and place in a bowl.
2. In a large sauté pan, melt the butter and add the spinach. Cook, turning frequently, until spinach is just

wilted. Allow to cool a few minutes. With the back of a spoon, press out excess liquid from the spinach. It is not necessary to press out all the liquid. Transfer to a mixing bowl.

3. Add the reserved pulp from the squash to the spinach, along with the ½ cup cheese, egg, oregano, garlic, parsley, salt, and pepper. Mix well. If mixture seems too wet, add 1–2 tablespoons bread crumbs.

4. Butter a baking dish. Fill the squash halves with the spinach mixture, mounding it slightly. Transfer the squash to a baking dish. Combine the ¼ cup Parmesan cheese and ¼ cup bread crumbs. Spread on the spinach. Drizzle a little olive oil over the top of each squash half.

5. Bake at 350 degrees for 15–20 minutes, or until the squash is just tender. Serves 4–6.

Grilled Plum Tomatoes

Look how simple this recipe is. I learned it from a chef who made huge trays of these tomatoes. When you taste this you will probably wonder, as I did, why didn't I ever try this myself? This is my idea of the way fast and fresh recipes should be. This is the way food should be, too.

15 plum tomatoes	*Salt and fresh pepper to*
5 tablespoons olive oil	*taste*

1. Cut the tomatoes in half lengthwise. Lay cut side up on a baking sheet. Brush each half with a teaspoon of olive oil. Add salt and pepper.

2. Run under the broiler, 2 inches from the unit, for 3 minutes, or until sizzling hot. Serves 4–6.

Variations

A little chopped garlic is good here also. Tomatoes can be baked at 350 degrees instead of broiling.

Tomatoes Stuffed with Rice

The big difference in this recipe is that is uses raw rice, eliminating extra cooking and burned fingers trying to get hot rice into a tomato. The only thing you have to worry about is filling the tomato three quarters full. More than that the stuffing expands over the top, runs down the side, and cooks into your favorite baking dish or oven, whichever is the harder to clean.

6 large ripe but firm
  tomatoes
6 tablespoons Italian
  rice
  Salt and fresh pepper
  to taste

1 small garlic clove,
  chopped
3 basil leaves, chopped
½ cup olive oil

1. Lay the tomatoes on a cutting board, stem end down. With a sharp knife, cut a lid ½ inch down on the top, but leave the lid hinged. Do not cut it off completely.
2. With a melon baller or grapefruit knife or spoon, scoop out the insides of each tomato. Place the pulp in a bowl. Sprinkle the inside of each tomato with a little salt.
3. Chop the pulp or process in a food processor. Return to the bowl and add the raw rice, salt, pepper, garlic, and basil. Add 3–4 tablespoons of olive oil. Mix thoroughly.
4. Place the mixture in the tomatoes, leaving a little space at the top for the rice to expand. If the mixture seems dry, add a spoonful of water to each tomato. Put the lids back in place.
5. Put the tomatoes in an oiled baking dish fairly close together. Sprinkle with olive oil. Place in a 350-degree oven and bake for 40–50 minutes, or until the rice is tender. Serve hot or at room temperature. Serves 4–6.

Zucchini Custards

2 tablespoons butter
1 cup grated zucchini,
  squeezed in a towel to
  remove moisture
2 tablespoons chopped
  onion
¼ teaspoon chopped
  oregano

2 eggs
2 egg yolks
1½ cups light cream
  Salt and fresh
  pepper to taste
  Butter for greasing
  molds

1. Melt the butter in a medium skillet. Add the zucchini and onion. Cook, stirring, 3–5 minutes. Add the oregano and set aside.
2. Whisk in a bowl the eggs, egg yolks, and cream. Add the salt and pepper and reserved zucchini mixture.
3. Butter six custard cups and spoon in zucchini mixture until two-thirds full. Set the molds in a water bath, allowing water to come halfway up the sides of the molds. Bake at 350 degrees for 20–25 minutes, or just until set. Let stand a few minutes, unmold, and serve. Serves 6.

Zucchini Fritters

 Oil for frying
2 cups grated zucchini
2 eggs, beaten
  Salt and fresh pepper
  to taste
1 tablespoon chopped
  flat-leaf parsley

1 teaspoon chopped
  marjoram
½ cup freshly grated
  Parmesan cheese
¾ cup flour

1. Heat 2 inches of oil to a temperature of 360 degrees.
2. Combine the zucchini, eggs, salt, pepper, parsley, mar-

joram, and cheese in a bowl. Add flour to bind the mixture.
3. Drop the mixture by teaspoonfuls into the hot oil and cook until brown on all sides. Remove with a slotted spoon to drain on brown paper. Serve hot or cold. Makes 2 dozen.

Note: The zucchini may be squeezed to release excess moisture, especially if the vegetable is old.

Zucchini with Garlic

I have a chef friend who says, "It's better to smell of garlic than to have bad breath." But if there is too much garlic here for your taste, cut it down a bit.

6 medium zucchini
½ cup olive oil
3 garlic cloves, chopped
Salt and fresh pepper
to taste

2 tablespoons chopped
flat-leaf parsley

1. Wash and dry the zucchini. Slice them thinly on a mandoline or in a food processor into julienne strips.
2. Heat the olive oil in a large skillet. When hot, add the garlic and stir it around with a wooden spatula for 1 minute.
3. Add the zucchini and toss over high heat for 3 minutes. Season with salt and pepper. Add the parsley and toss to distribute the seasonings. Serves 4–6.

Scallion Fritters

A specialty from Chef Capurro of the Manuelina restaurant in Recco, near Genoa.

½ cup plus 2
  tablespoons flour
½ teaspoon baking
  powder
½ teaspoon salt
1 egg

1 cup sliced scallions,
  using some of the
  green part
⅓ cup diced green
  pepper
Oil for frying

1. Place the flour, baking powder, and salt in a bowl.
2. In another bowl, beat the egg with a whisk until thick.
   Continue beating while adding the flour mixture, a little
   at a time. Add the sliced scallions and diced green
   pepper. This is a medium to stiff batter.
3. In the meantime, heat the oil slowly to 370 degrees.
   Use a thermometer or test with a cube of bread. If the
   bread turns golden brown in a minute, start frying.
4. Drop the batter from a tablespoon, allowing 5–6 small
   fritters to cook at a time. Use a slotted spoon to turn
   fritters while cooking. When delicate brown, remove
   with a slotted spoon. Drain on heavy brown paper.
   Keep warm in a 200-degree oven until all the fritters
   are cooked. Sprinkle lightly with salt. Serves 4–6.

Baked Spinach I

1 pound spinach,
  washed and stems
  removed
1 container (15 ounces)
  ricotta cheese
½ cup freshly grated
  Parmesan cheese

⅓ cup flour
1 egg, beaten
Touch of grated
  nutmeg
Salt and fresh pepper
  to taste
2 tablespoons butter

1. Cook the spinach in a small amount of water until
   tender; drain. Squeeze to remove excess moisture and
   chop finely.

2. In a large bowl, combine the ricotta, ¼ cup Parmesan, flour, egg, nutmeg, salt, pepper, and chopped spinach; mix well. Spread evenly in a 9-inch pie dish.
3. Sprinkle with remaining Parmesan cheese and dot with butter. Bake at 350 degrees 30 minutes or until browned on top. Cool slightly before serving. Serves 6–8.

Baked Spinach II

4 tablespoons butter
4 cups fresh spinach, washed and stems removed
1 cup ricotta cheese
3 eggs, lightly beaten
¼ cup freshly grated Parmesan cheese
½ cup heavy cream
¼ cup toasted pine nuts (see note)
Salt and fresh pepper to taste
Grated nutmeg to taste

1. Heat the butter in a saucepan and, when the foam subsides, add the spinach. Cook until the spinach wilts, stirring constantly with a wooden spatula.
2. Press out excess moisture. Place in a bowl and add the ricotta, eggs, Parmesan, cream, and nuts. Mix well and season with salt, pepper, and a touch of nutmeg.
3. Place in a 9-inch baking dish. Bake at 350 degrees for 20–25 minutes, or until set. Serves 4.

Note: To toast pine nuts, lay them on a baking sheet. Bake 10 minutes at 350 degrees.

Spinach with Garlic

3 pounds spinach, washed and stems removed
½ cup chicken stock
2 garlic cloves, 1 whole and 1 chopped
3 tablespoons olive oil
Salt and fresh pepper to taste
Lemon wedges for garnish

1. Place the spinach in a saucepan with water clinging to it. Add the stock and whole clove of garlic. Place lid on spinach to steam for 5 minutes, or until wilted.

2. Remove the lid and discard the garlic. Drain the spinach in a colander or sieve and chop coarsely.

3. Heat the olive oil in a sauté pan. Add the chopped garlic, salt, pepper, and spinach. Cook until hot. Serve with lemon wedges. Serves 4–6.

4

SOUPS

In Italy, my favorite soup is minestrone, a thick vegetable soup with pasta or rice.

But that's like saying my favorite food is food. In America, when you order vegetable soup in a restaurant you're always more or less sure of what you're going to eat. Order minestrone in Italy and you're sure of nothing, except a surprise. I've had minestrone with and without rice, pasta, and dried beans; minestrones that were light and elegant little vegetable bisques and minestrones that would float a spoon—and the knife and fork and sugar bowl, too, if you put them in there.

Italian soups seem to have more regional variations than any other food. And more personal variations, too.

Italian soups have as their main ingredient imagination.

And Italian soups are fast. Of course, given the time limits of this book, I've left out soups that call for long soaking of legumes, but almost any Italian soup can be made quickly and easily in well under an hour. Italian broths are lighter—so light that when I first started teach-

ing at the Gritti I asked for a few pieces of chicken on
the side whenever I asked the kitchen for chicken stock.
And then made my own stock a little stronger. As time
went on I got more and more used to this delicate Italian
brodo, and maybe you will too. If not, dump in more
chicken, and cook it the way you like it.

Any of these soups can make a good first course or,
with a salad, a light supper. In Italy, you would never eat
a soup with noodles and a pasta course at the same meal.
Even in Italy, people believe it is possible to have too
many noodles.

Chicken Stock

Many of the soups in this chapter call for chicken stock,
and this one is especially well flavored.

4 pounds chicken backs,
   wings, and necks, or 1
   4-pound chicken
1 cup sliced carrots
1 cup sliced celery
2 large onions, peeled
   and quartered
2 whole cloves

Salt and fresh pepper
   to taste
1 cup dry white wine
1 garlic clove, mashed
Few sprigs fresh thyme
1 bay leaf
Few sprigs parsley

1. Place all the ingredients in a large kettle. Cover with
water, about 4 quarts. Bring to a boil slowly and skim
off any scum. Partially cover and cook gently for 1½
hours.

2. Strain through a fine sieve. For extra strong stock, reduce further to intensify the flavor. Makes 2–3 quarts.

Asparagus Soup

8 tablespoons butter
2 large onions, chopped
3 medium potatoes, peeled and cut into chunks
2 pounds asparagus, cut into 2 inch pieces, tips removed and reserved

4 cups chicken stock
Salt and fresh pepper to taste
2 cups heavy cream
¼ cup freshly grated Parmesan cheese

1. Melt the butter in a large saucepan. Add the onion and cook, stirring, until wilted, about 3 minutes.
2. Add the potatoes and asparagus pieces, reserving the tips, and stir 1 minute.
3. Add the stock. If it does not cover the vegetables, add some water. Add salt and pepper. Cover and bring to a boil. Reduce heat to a simmer and cook, partially covered, for 20 minutes, or until the vegetables are tender. Purée in a food mill and return to the saucepan.
4. Add the cream and asparagus tips and bring to a boil. Sprinkle with Parmesan cheese and serve. Serves 6.

Note: A food mill works best here for puréeing because sometimes the skin on the asparagus can be tough.

Minestrone

1 tablespoon olive oil
4 ounces salt pork,
  diced
1 large onion,
  chopped
1 large carrot,
  chopped
1 celery rib, chopped
2 medium potatoes,
  diced
2 small green
  peppers, seeded and
  diced
2–3 garlic cloves, finely
  chopped
2 tablespoons tomato
  paste
4 tomatoes, peeled,
  seeded, and chopped

2 quarts chicken stock
Salt and fresh pepper
  to taste
Few fresh basil
  leaves, chopped
2 tablespoons chopped
  flat-leaf parsley
¾ cup ditalini, or other
  small soup pasta
½ pound fresh spinach,
  washed and trimmed
  of stems
½ cup freshly grated
  Parmesan cheese,
  plus additional cheese
  for each serving

1. Heat the oil in a large soup pot. Add the salt pork and fry until crisp.
2. Add the onion, carrot, celery, potatoes, and green pepper. Sauté 4–5 minutes, stirring frequently.
3. Add the garlic and sauté 2 minutes longer.
4. Add the tomato paste, tomatoes, and chicken stock. Add salt, pepper, basil, and parsley and bring to a boil. Reduce to a simmer, partially cover, and cook 30 minutes, or until the vegetables are just tender.
5. After 20 minutes, add the pasta. Add the spinach and ½ cup cheese 5 minutes before the soup is ready to serve. Serve with additional Parmesan cheese on each serving. Serve hot or at room temperature. Serves 8–10.

Variations

Instead of spinach, add ½ small head of cabbage, shredded.

Add 1 cup fresh peas and/or 2 or 3 small zucchini, diced.

Add cannellini (dried white beans) or rice instead of potato.

Spoon extra virgin oil over each serving.

Use water instead of chicken stock.

Add a spoonful of pesto (see page 113) to each serving.

Add a bit of gremolata (see page 108) to each serving.

Eggplant Soup

This soup is not very pretty. In fact, the real reason for the tomato julienne is to make it look a little better—or at least not so awful. But wait until you taste it. Beauty is only skin deep. And you don't eat the skin of soup.

2 slices bacon, cut into
    small pieces
1 large eggplant (1
    pound or more),
    peeled and cut into
    cubes
2 celery ribs, sliced
1 carrot, peeled and
    sliced
2 tablespoons butter
4 cups fresh chicken
    stock

2 tablespoons chopped
    flat-leaf parsley
1 tablespoon chopped
    scallion
    Salt and fresh pepper
    to taste
2 cups heavy cream
1 skinned, seeded
    tomato cut into
    julienne strips

1. Cook the bacon in a large pan on medium-high heat.
2. Add the eggplant, sliced celery, carrot, and butter. Stir to coat all the vegetables.
3. Add the chicken stock, parsley, scallion, salt, and pepper. Cover and simmer for 30 minutes.
4. Remove from the heat and purée in a food mill, using the finest blade. Return soup to the pan and add the cream. Taste for seasoning. If a thinner soup is desired, add more stock. Serve in hot bowls and top with tomato julienne. Serves 4–6.

Zucchini Soup

This soup is a favorite in mid-summer when zucchini is plentiful.

6 tablespoons butter
2 medium onions, chopped
2 potatoes, peeled and chopped
1 celery rib, chopped
12 medium zucchini, washed and chopped

8 cups chicken stock, or more
2 tablespoons chopped flat-leaf parsley
Salt and fresh pepper to taste
6 basil leaves, chopped
1 cup heavy cream

1. Heat the butter in a large saucepan. When the foam subsides, add the onions and cook 3 minutes, stirring with a wooden spatula.
2. Add the potatoes and celery and cook another 3 minutes.
3. Add the zucchini and stir to mix. Pour on enough chicken stock to cover. Add the parsley, salt, and pepper. Bring to a boil. Turn to a simmer and cook about 25 minutes.
4. Purée the soup in batches in a blender or food processor, or use a food mill. Add the basil and cream. Adjust seasoning. Serve hot or cold. To chill quickly, stir soup over ice. Serves 8–10.

Cream of Onion Soup

This version of cream of onion soup comes from Harry's Bar in Venice. Harry's is loaded with Americans in the tourist season, who all come there for the real American food—and who all usually wind up eating the real Italian food on the menu. This soup is not Italian, and not particularly American either, just pure Harry's Bar. And delicious.

8 tablespoons butter
6 cups sliced onions
1 garlic clove, chopped
1 cup chopped celery
2 cups peeled and diced
  potato
6–8 cups chicken stock

2 cups light cream
  Salt and fresh
  pepper to taste
2 tablespoons
  chopped flat-leaf
  parsley

1. Melt the butter in a large saucepan. When the foam subsides, stir in the onions, garlic, celery, and potato. Cook on low heat, stirring with a spatula. Do not allow the onions to brown.
2. Pour enough stock over the onions to cover and cook slowly, covered, for about 20 minutes.
3. Add the cream, salt, and pepper. Purée the mixture in a food processor or blender. Serve hot or cold garnished with parsley. Serves 6–8.

Spinach and Chicken Soup

Any available green may be used in place of the spinach, especially swiss chard tops, escarole, or lettuce.

6–8 cups chicken stock
1 pound spinach,
   washed, stems
   removed, and
   julienned
1½ cups cooked
   chicken (optional)
   Salt and fresh pepper
   to taste

Freshly grated
   nutmeg to taste
1 teaspoon grated
   lemon rind
¼ cup freshly grated
   Parmesan cheese

Bring the chicken stock to a boil. Reduce the heat and add the spinach, chicken, salt, pepper, nutmeg, and lemon rind. Heat through 3–4 minutes. Serve with the Parmesan sprinkled over. Serves 4–6.

Sweet Red Pepper Soup

An unusual delicate flavor, and a beautiful color. It makes a festive first course served hot or cold. And when the main course has a sort of thrown-together look, this soup makes everything else seem a little more elegant.

8 tablespoons butter
2 cups chopped leeks,
   white part only, or
   chopped onion
2 garlic cloves, chopped
4 cups chopped red
   peppers
2 tablespoons flour

2 cups chicken stock
   Salt and fresh pepper
   to taste
2 cups light cream
2 cups yogurt
2 tablespoons chopped
   basil

1. Melt the butter in a large kettle. When the foam subsides, add the leeks and garlic. Stir with a wooden spatula to coat well with butter. Cook 3 minutes.
2. Add the peppers and continue to cook and stir for another 3 minutes.
3. Add the flour and cook until it disappears.

4. Add the chicken stock and let it come to a boil. Season with salt and pepper.
5. Purée the soup in a blender or food processor. Return to the pan and add the cream, yogurt, and chopped basil. Bring to a boil. Serve hot or stir over ice to chill and serve cold. Serves 8–10.

Note: I've made this with buttermilk instead of yogurt and cream for an interesting taste.

Potato Soup

This soup recipe was given to me by a Neapolitan friend. More garlic can be added for a more assertive flavor.

6 slices bacon, cut up
4 tablespoons chopped
  flat-leaf parsley
2 garlic cloves, chopped
8 cups chicken stock
6 medium potatoes,
  peeled and diced

Salt and fresh pepper
to taste
Grated Parmesan
cheese

1. In large saucepan, cook the bacon until crisp.
2. Add the parsley and garlic and cook 3 minutes.
3. Add the chicken stock and potatoes. Bring to a boil, reduce the heat, and simmer 15–20 minutes, or until potatoes are just tender. Season with salt and pepper. If soup is too thick, thin with chicken stock. Serve sprinkled with Parmesan cheese. Serves 6.

Potato and Scallion Soup

4 medium potatoes
8 cups chicken stock
  Salt and fresh
  pepper to taste

4–5 tablespoons
  chopped scallions

1. Peel and julienne the potatoes, but do not soak them in water. The starch is necessary to give a little body to the soup.
2. Bring the stock to a boil in a large saucepan. Add the potatoes, salt, and pepper. Simmer, partially covered, 10 minutes, or until the potatoes are just tender.
3. Remove the cover and add the scallions. Cook 3 minutes longer. Serves 4–6.

Yellow Squash Soup with Chicken

8 cups chicken stock
1 small chicken breast, skinned and split in two
4 tablespoons butter
1 large onion, chopped
1 garlic clove, chopped
8–10 small yellow squash, washed and diced
2 medium potatoes, peeled and diced
1 teaspoon chopped rosemary
Salt and fresh pepper to taste
2 tablespoons chopped flat-leaf parsley

1. Heat the chicken stock and simmer the chicken breast in it for 15 minutes.
2. Heat the butter in a saucepan. When the foam subsides, add the onion and garlic. Cook, while stirring with a wooden spatula, for 3 minutes.
3. Add the squash and potatoes and stir for 2 more minutes.
4. Remove the chicken breast from the stock and dice. Pour the stock into the squash pan. Cook on moderate heat, covered, until the vegetables are tender, 15 minutes.
5. Add the rosemary, salt, pepper, and diced chicken. Bring gently to a boil. Add parsley and serve hot or cold. Serves 6–8.

Variation

Substitute zucchini for yellow squash.

Mushroom Consommé

2 ounces dried Italian
  mushrooms
1½ quarts chicken stock
3 tablespoons butter
½ pound fresh
  mushrooms,
  chopped

Salt and fresh pepper
  to taste
4 tablespoons dry
  Marsala

1. Soak the dried mushrooms in hot water to cover for 15 minutes. Drain and chop.
2. Heat the stock in a saucepan with the chopped dried mushrooms.
3. Melt the butter in a small sauté pan. Add the fresh mushrooms and cook 3 minutes, stirring. Add to the stock mixture. Simmer 30 minutes with the pan partially covered. Season with salt and pepper to taste. Strain, if desired, and stir in the Marsala. Serves 6.

Tomato Onion Soup

3 tablespoons oil
1 garlic clove, chopped
4 large onions, roughly
  chopped
1 large celery rib, sliced
1 large carrot, chopped
8–10 tomatoes, peeled
  and chopped

6 cups chicken stock
¼ cup parsley leaves
2 bay leaves
  Salt and fresh
  pepper
  Thinly sliced
  scallions

1. Heat the oil in a saucepan. When hot, add the garlic, onions, celery, and carrot and cook 3–5 minutes.
2. Add the tomatoes, chicken stock, parsley, bay leaves, salt, and pepper. Cover and simmer 30 minutes. Remove the bay leaves.
3. Purée in a food mill, using the finest blade. Serve with sliced scallions on top. Serves 4–6.

Note: Thin with more stock if soup is too thick.

Quick Uncooked Tomato Soup

This soup is not only simply made but has a lovely fresh tomato taste.

8 large tomatoes, peeled, seeded, and chopped
¼ cup chopped scallions
Salt and fresh pepper
3–4 basil leaves, chopped

2 cups chicken stock
2 tablespoons chopped flat-leaf parsley
2 cups cream, light or heavy

Combine all the ingredients except cream in a blender or food processor. Purée until smooth. Add the cream and stir to blend. Add more cream if too thick. Serves 6–8.

Fresh Tomato Soup

A spoonful of pesto changes the flavor of this soup.

2 tablespoons butter
1 large onion,
  chopped
2 celery ribs, chopped
8 tomatoes, cut into
  quarters
4–5 basil leaves,
  chopped

1 bay leaf
2 tablespoons chopped
  flat-leaf parsley
6 cups chicken stock
Juice of ½ lemon
Salt and fresh pepper
  to taste

1. Melt the butter in a large saucepan. When the foam subsides, add the onion and celery. Cook 5 minutes, stirring with a wooden spatula.
2. Add the tomatoes. Crush them against the side of the pan with the wooden spatula. Cook 10–15 minutes, stirring occasionally.
3. Add the basil, bay leaf, parsley, and stock. Cover and cook another 10–15 minutes. Remove the bay leaf.
4. Purée the soup through the finest blade of a food mill. Add the lemon juice, salt, and pepper and serve hot or cold. Serves 4–6.

Note: To purée in a food processor or blender, remove the skin and seeds from the tomatoes before cooking.

Fresh Tomato Bouillon

2 tablespoons butter
1 large onion,
  chopped
2 large celery ribs,
  chopped
8 large tomatoes,
  quartered
5–6 large basil leaves,
  chopped

½ cup parsley leaves
1 bay leaf
6 cups strong chicken
  stock
Salt and fresh pepper
  to taste
Toasted bread cubes
  or croutons for
  garnish

1. Melt the butter in a large saucepan. Add the onion and celery and cook 5 minutes.
2. Add the tomatoes, basil, parsley, and bay leaf. Cover the pan and bring to a boil. Reduce the heat to a simmer and cook for 30 minutes. Remove and discard bay leaf.
3. Remove from the heat and purée the soup in a food mill with the finest blade. Return to the pan, add the chicken stock, and heat. Season with salt and pepper. Serve with croutons. Serves 4–6.

Celery Rice Soup

8 cups chicken stock
  Salt and fresh pepper
  to taste
1 cup Italian rice
6–8 celery ribs, thinly
  sliced on the
  diagonal

4 tablespoons thinly
  sliced scallions

1. Bring the stock to a boil in a large saucepan. Add salt, pepper, rice, and celery. Simmer, partially covered, until the rice and celery are just tender, 15–20 minutes.
2. Add the scallions and simmer, uncovered, 3 minutes. Serves 4–6.

Note: The rice somewhat thickens the stock and gives it body.

Italian Cheese Soup

4 tablespoons butter
2 carrots, peeled and
  sliced
1 onion, chopped
2 celery ribs, chopped
1 small green pepper,
  chopped

6 cups chicken stock
¾ cup coarsely grated
  provolone cheese
  Salt and fresh pepper
  to taste
¼ cup freshly grated
  Parmesan cheese

1. Melt the butter in a saucepan. Add the carrots, onion, celery, and green pepper. Cook, while stirring with a wooden spatula, for 5 minutes.
2. Add the chicken stock, partially cover, and cook for 10 minutes, or until the vegetables are tender.
3. Purée in a food processor, blender, or a food mill. Return to low heat and add the provolone. Heat just to melt the cheese. Stir. Add salt and pepper. Sprinkle Parmesan cheese over the top just before serving. Serves 6.

Chicken Soup with Egg and Parmesan

3 tablespoons freshly
  grated Parmesan
  cheese
2 tablespoons chopped
  flat-leaf parsley

3 eggs, beaten
6 cups chicken stock
  Salt and fresh pepper
  to taste

In a small bowl, stir the cheese and parsley into the eggs. Bring the stock to a boil. Pour the egg mixture into the stock in a thin stream, stirring constantly until the eggs are set. Season with salt and pepper. Serves 4–6.

Chicken Liver Soup

4 tablespoons butter
½ pound chicken
  livers, cleaned and
  sliced
  Salt and fresh
  pepper to taste
6–8 cups chicken stock

½ cup small pasta
1 cup fresh small peas
2 tablespoons finely
  chopped flat-leaf
  parsley
½ cup freshly grated
  Parmesan cheese

1. Melt the butter in a large saucepan. Add the livers and
   sauté 3 minutes, or until no longer pink. Season with
   salt and pepper.
2. Pour the chicken stock over the livers. Add the pasta
   and peas and cook until pasta is barely tender. Sprinkle
   the parsley and cheese over and serve. Serves 4–6.

Pasta and Bean Soup

In northern Italy, red beans are added to this soup; in the
south, white beans are the custom.

6 tablespoons olive oil
¼ pound pancetta or
  blanched bacon,
  diced
2 garlic cloves, chopped
1 onion, chopped
2 celery ribs, chopped
3 cups shelled lima
  beans
3 cups shelled fresh
  cranberry beans

2 tablespoons chopped
  flat-leaf parsley
1 cup tomato chunks
1 tablespoon chopped
  fresh rosemary
8 cups light chicken
  stock
  Salt and fresh pepper
  to taste
2 cups ditalini or other
  small soup pasta

1. Heat the oil in a large kettle and sauté the pancetta.
2. Add the garlic, onion, and celery. Cook, while stirring
   with a wooden spatula, until soft, 3–5 minutes.
3. Add the beans, parsley, tomatoes, rosemary, and stock.
   Bring to a boil. Add salt and pepper. Turn to a simmer
   and cook 20 minutes.
4. Remove half the beans and purée them in blender, food
   processor, or food mill. Return the purée to the kettle.
5. Add the pasta and cook until the pasta is al dente, 5–
   10 minutes. Serve hot with a pepper mill and cruet of
   olive oil on the side. Serves 6–8.

Note: This soup is frequently served at room temperature, but I prefer it hot. Parmesan cheese may be sprinkled over the soup, but I prefer it just with the olive oil and freshly ground pepper.

Italian Fish Soup

Cioppino probably derived from this soup made by immigrants from Genoa who opened fish restaurants on the San Francisco waterfront and, as always, began to develop new recipes.

3–4 pounds assorted
    fish fillets, such as
    bass, snapper,
    halibut, etc.
    Fish heads and
    bones
  6 cups water
    Salt and fresh
    pepper to taste
  2 large onions, finely
    chopped
    Few sprigs fresh
    thyme

  1 bay leaf
  ½ cup olive oil
2–3 garlic cloves,
    chopped
  1 cup dry white wine
4–5 tomatoes, peeled,
    seeded, and
    chopped
  ½ cup chopped flat-
    leaf parsley
  ¼ teaspoon saffron

1. Cut the fish into chunks.
2. Cook the heads, bones, and any trimmings in water with salt, pepper, ½ cup chopped onion, thyme, and bay leaf over medium heat for ½ hour. Strain and reserve the stock.
3. Heat the oil in a saucepan. Add the rest of the onion and garlic and sauté, while stirring with a wooden spatula, for 3–5 minutes.
4. Add the fish. Carefully sauté for a minute on each side.

5. Add the wine, tomatoes, parsley, and strained stock and bring to a boil. Add the saffron. Partially cover and simmer over low heat for 10 minutes. Season with salt and pepper. Serve hot. Serves 6.

Variation

Shrimp, clams, mussels, and squid can be added to this soup.

Clam Soup

2 cups dry white wine or
  vermouth
1 bay leaf
3 quarts clams, cleaned
3 tablespoons butter
2 white onions, chopped
1 garlic clove, chopped

3 cups water
1 cup milk
  Salt and fresh pepper
  to taste
1 cup heavy cream
3 egg yolks

1. In a large pot, bring the wine and bay leaf to a boil. Reduce the heat and add the clams. Cover, raise the heat, and cook 4–5 minutes until clams open. Shake or stir the clams while cooking. Strain through a very fine sieve. Reserve the juices and remove clams from the shells.
2. Heat the butter in a large pot. Add the onions and cook 3 minutes. Add the garlic and cook 2 minutes longer. Add the reserved liquid, water, and milk. Simmer 10 minutes. Add salt and pepper.
3. Whisk together the cream and egg yolks. Whisk into the soup. Add the clams. Reheat but do not boil. Serves 6.

Mussel Soup

THE STOCK

1 pound fish bones,
rinsed
2 celery ribs, chopped
roughly
1 onion, chopped
roughly

Salt and fresh
pepper to taste
4–5 sprigs parsley
1 bay leaf
5–6 cups water

THE MUSSELS

1½ cups dry white wine
1 bay leaf
4 quarts mussels,
washed, scraped, and
beards removed
2 tablespoons butter
2 celery ribs, chopped

2 leeks, cleaned and
chopped (or white
onion)
2 carrots, peeled and
chopped
Salt and fresh pepper
1 cup heavy cream

1. Combine all the ingredients for the stock in a saucepan. Bring to a boil. Reduce to a simmer, partially cover, and simmer 20 minutes. Skim, if needed. Strain and set aside.
2. In a large stock pot, bring the wine and bay leaf to a boil. Add the cleaned mussels. Cover and cook 3–5 minutes, or until the mussels open. Stir or shake the pan during cooking.
3. Melt the butter in a large sauté pan. Add the celery, leeks, and carrots. Stir to mix. Cover with a round piece of wax paper. Reduce the heat and cook 10 minutes.
4. Strain the mussels, reserving the steaming liquid. Remove the mussels from the shells and set aside.
5. Combine the mussel liquid, strained fish stock, and vegetable mixture in a large pot. Simmer 15 minutes. Add salt and pepper if needed. Add the mussels and heavy cream. Reheat. Serves 8–10.

5

PASTA

PASTA MAY BE THE PERFECT FOOD. IT IS HEALTHY, NOUR-
ishing, inexpensive, easy to cook, goes with just about
anything, and is a feature of many different cuisines in
widely different parts of the world.

Besides all that, pasta is . . . soothing. Whenever you're
lost in the kitchen with nothing in the house for dinner,
you can always rely on pasta. I love it—and I love to
make it, fresh, from flour and eggs.

But I don't like to see pasta turning into a fussy and
pretentious food fad.

So let me say again, there is nothing wrong with boxed
pasta. Millions of Italians eat boxed pasta every day.
Thousands of restaurants, large and small, cheap or elegant, serve it with every imaginable sauce. In fact, it
seems to be that in Italy, seafood sauces are usually served
with boxed pasta rather than fresh—from preference.

If you have one of those shops that specialize in making
pasta in your area—and they seem to be springing up all
over the place—custom-made pasta is also excellent. It

cooks faster than the boxed, a pound seems to go farther, and it looks very pretty on the plate. In New York, as in California, many restaurants where the waiter assures you that the pasta is "made fresh today" serve pasta made fresh at a pasta shop. You can use this pasta yourself, interchangeably with homemade pasta, just as those restaurants do.

You can also make your own pasta. This is not a long and tedious process. Anyone who can make pastry dough can make pasta. Kids can make pasta. It's easy, and fun, like playing with play-dough. Remember that peasant women in Italy have been making pasta for centuries, with inferior flour, with tiny eggs or with no eggs at all, with nothing but a board and a rolling pin. Pasta is not hard to make. There is not even a trick to it. As you do in making a pie shell or bread, you will acquire a feel for the dough and realize when you need a little more flour or an extra egg because of the weather or the temperature. But you will make perfectly acceptable pasta the first time, and only get better as you go along. So the way to learn to make pasta is—just make it. Plow right in. There'll always be noodles when you're finished, and they'll always taste good with your sauce.

One of the fussiest of the new pasta fads is the insistence on hand-rolled noodles. I have heard it claimed that hand-rolled noodles—rolled on wood, nothing else— are porous and absorb sauce, while pasta rolled through a pasta machine's steel rollers is slick, so sauce runs right off.

This may be true.

But I say if you have guests in your home who spend their time appraising the slipperiness of your pasta and sauces, then you should feed them french fries and be done with it. People who love pasta don't sit down to examine it. They sit down to eat. I have rolled out pasta on my slate-top table, on a Formica countertop, and I am sure I could roll it out on a linoleum floor if I had to.

But in all the classes conducted by Italian chefs at the

Gritti Palace, only one rolled out pasta by hand. And he only did it to show how it could be done. Back in his own kitchen in his own restaurant he didn't hand-roll pasta. As in every other restaurant kitchen I visited, he had a big pasta machine, a professional version of the hand-cranked machine you can buy for your own kitchen, with the same steel rollers.

The only pasta I find unacceptable is the kind produced by those machines where you put flour and eggs in one end and pasta is extruded out the other. To me, the pasta always had an off-taste and texture, and the darn things are so hard to clean you don't wind up saving any time anyway.

Some recipes for pasta make a mystique of forming the flour into a mound, making a well in the center, breaking the eggs into the hole, delicately mixing with a fork, turning the flour carefully from the bottom of the mound, kneading at least twenty or exactly eighteen minutes...

I like to throw all the ingredients into my food processor.

And my way works.

So if you've ever made bread—or never made bread—you can follow these recipes and be sure of making good pasta. Good the first time. Better the second time. Perfect the third.

Included in this section are more than thirty recipes for pasta sauces. These are a guide, as there is always something in the refrigerator to put over pasta, even if it is simply butter and cheese, or olive oil, garlic, and parsley. Look in the vegetable chapter for ideas. Many of those dishes may be tossed with pasta, as may some of the appetizer or salad ideas. The pasta on which you put your sauce can be any kind. Next time you go to the market examine all the different shapes, and choose the one you like best. They range in size from the tiny pastina or orzo all the way up to the big tubes for manicotti. We are fortunate today to have all the various shapes. Women years ago made their own pasta, and some still do in remote areas, with all kinds of gadgets to change the shapes. Garganelli, a macaroni type with ridges, were rolled on a comblike gadget available now at country fairs in Italy. Pasta was cut on a gadget that looked like a guitar, called a chitarra. It was stamped out in rounds, each with a design, called corzetti. It was rolled out with a grooved brass rolling pin to make troccoli. Unfortunately, in a fast and fresh book we have no time for these.

Food Processor Pasta

3 cups unbleached all-
   purpose flour
4 eggs

1 teaspoon salt
1–2 tablespoons olive oil

1. Put the flour in the bowl of a food processor fitted with the steel blade.
2. Beat the eggs, salt, and oil together. Pour the egg mixture through the feed tube of the processor using on and off pulses.
3. When the mixture looks like coarse meal, turn it out on a floured board. Knead it for a few minutes until it forms a ball.
4. Roll the dough into a sausage shape. Cut into 6 pieces and flatten each piece. Flour each piece. Crank one piece through the pasta machine with the rollers opened to the widest opening. Fold the dough in half and crank through until smooth, 6–8 times.
5. Set the rollers to the next descending number and repeat. Continue to roll the dough through until 1/16-inch thick, or down to the last notch. Repeat with the rest of the dough. If sticky at any time, dust with flour, Well-made sheets of pasta should have the feel of chamois. Dough is now ready to be cut. Makes 1½ pounds

Variations

Spinach pasta. Add 6 ounces of spinach, chopped, cooked, drained, and squeezed of all liquid, to the eggs.

Beet pasta. Add ¼ cup puréed beets, well drained, to the eggs.

Watercress pasta. Remove leaves from 1 large bunch watercress. Purée in a food processor or chop with a knife. Add to the eggs.

Broccoli pasta. Add 6 ounces puréed cooked broccoli to the eggs.

Mint pasta. Add ¼ cup chopped fresh mint leaves to the eggs.

Herb pasta. Add ¼ cup chopped fresh herbs of your choice, basil, rosemary, or oregano, to the eggs.

Parsley pasta. Add ¼ cup chopped fresh parsley to the eggs.

Saffron pasta. Dissolve 1–2 teaspoons powdered saffron in the eggs. Don't add too much saffron or the pasta will have a medicinal taste.

Carrot pasta. Add ½ cup puréed cooked carrots to the eggs.

Roasted red pepper pasta. Purée 1 or 2 roasted peppers (skins and seeds removed) and add to the eggs.

Chocolate pasta. Add 4 tablespoons powdered cocoa to the flour.

To Cut Pasta

Hand-cranked machines and electric roller pasta machines are equipped with a set of cutters, which are for two widths of noodles: one for fettuccine or regular noodles, and one for fine noodles, or tagliarini. Attach the cutters to the machine and cut as desired. If dough sticks at any time, simply flour both sides of the pasta. Place the cut noodles on baking sheets lined with towels coated with flour or semolina. Toss them in the air frequently. Some chefs let the noodles dry before cooking. Nowadays, the young chefs I know do not let the noodles dry at all— they cover them with a damp cloth until ready to cook.

To Cook Pasta

For each pound of pasta to be cooked, bring 6–8 quarts of water to a brisk boil. Just before adding the pasta, season with 1 tablespoon coarse salt, preferably sea salt. No oil! Lower the pasta into the boiling water. Stir it occasionally with a wooden fork to keep it from sticking together. For homemade pasta, cook for 2–3 minutes. For boxed pasta, cook for 5 minutes and then start testing it by biting a strand. Fresh pasta is thin, soft, cools quickly, and can't be *al dente*, or still have a bite to it. But boxed pasta can. Cooking time depends upon the size and shape of the pasta. The second the pasta is cooked to your likeness, drain it in a large sieve or colander. Immediately toss the pasta with the desired sauce. Do not oversauce the pasta. Serve immediately.

Cannelloni

½ recipe for homemade pasta, rolled in machine (see page 90)
2 tablespoons melted butter
8 ounces cream cheese
8 ounces ricotta cheese
¼ cup freshly grated Parmesan cheese
1 small garlic clove, chopped

1 egg
Salt and fresh pepper to taste
1 cup chopped spinach
1 cup tomato sauce I (see page 102)
½ cup freshly grated Parmesan cheese

1. Cut the pasta dough into 3- by 4-inch rectangles. Cook a few at a time in boiling salted water for 2 minutes. Remove from the water with tongs and lay the pieces on wet marble or a wet Formica countertop.
2. Brush each piece of cooked pasta with melted butter.
3. Combine the cream cheese, ricotta, ¼ cup Parmesan, garlic, egg, salt, pepper, and spinach. Mix well and spread on each piece of pasta.
4. Roll up lightly. Place seam down in a buttered baking dish containing a spoonful of tomato sauce. Spread the remaining sauce on top of the cannelloni. Sprinkle with ½ cup Parmesan cheese and bake at 350 degrees for 20–30 minutes. Serves 6.

Note: Spread ½ cup medium béchamel sauce (see page 102) over the tomato sauce for a richer dish.

Ricotta Cheese Stuffing for Pasta

1 pound ricotta cheese,
or ½ pound ricotta
cheese and ½ pound
cream cheese
¼ cup freshly grated
Parmesan cheese
2 egg yolks

¼ cup diced prosciutto
1 tablespoon chopped
flat-leaf parsley
Salt and fresh pepper
to taste
Tomato sauce I or II
(see pages 102–103)

Combine all the ingredients except tomato sauce in a bowl and spread on or stuff cooked pasta. Serve with tomato sauce on top. Enough filling for 20 jumbo shells, 8–10 manicotti shells, 8–10 cannelloni rectangles.

Note: Manicotti is one of those popular American pasta dishes seldom seen in Italy except from Naples south. The tubes are usually stuffed with this mixture and topped with tomato sauce.

Lasagne

1 pound ricotta or
cottage cheese
8 ounces cream cheese
1 egg
3 tablespoons heavy
cream
1 cup freshly grated
Parmesan cheese
2 tablespoons chopped
flat-leaf parsley

Salt and fresh pepper
to taste
½ pound wide lasagne
noodles, cooked as
for pasta (see pages
92–3)
Bolognese sauce (see
page 105)
8 ounces mozzarella
cheese, thinly sliced

1. Blend together the ricotta or cottage cheese and cream cheese. When very smooth, add the egg, cream, ¼ cup of the grated Parmesan cheese, parsley, and some salt and pepper to taste. Beat until thoroughly blended.

2. Spread a generous spoonful of this mixture on each piece of lasagne, smooth with a spatula, and roll. Place in a shallow baking dish that can be used for serving. Spoon the bolgonese sauce over and top with thin slices of mozzarella cheese. Sprinkle with the remaining ¾ cup of grated Parmesan cheese.
3. Bake at 375 degrees until thoroughly heated and lightly browned, 20–30 minutes. Serve in the baking dish. Serves 6–8.

Note: These lasagne noodles are attractive if you stand them on end in the serving dish. This dish can also be prepared by layering the pasta, putting béchamel, meat sauce, and Parmesan cheese between the layers.

Lasagne Mold

Oil for greasing mold
11 pieces cooked lasagne noodles
3 cups cooked green noodles
1½ cups medium béchamel sauce (see page 102)
1 cup ricotta cheese, drained
4 eggs
2 tablespoons chopped flat-leaf parsley
Salt and fresh pepper to taste

1. Oil a 6–8 cup ring mold. Line the mold with overlapping pieces of lasagne. Let the ends of the lasagne hang over the edge and the hole in the center of the mold.
2. In a large bowl, mix the cooked noodles with the béchamel sauce.
3. Mix together the ricotta cheese and eggs. Add to the noodles. Add the parsley, salt, and pepper. Mix well and fill the mold. Fold the edges of the lasagne over the mixture. Cover with a piece of buttered wax paper and bake in a 350-degree oven 40 minutes, or until set.

4. Loosen with the point of a thin knife or spatula. Let set a few minutes before unmolding onto a round serving dish. Serve with sage butter (page 197), tomato sauce I or II (pages 102–103) or melted butter and Parmesan cheese. Serves 8.

Spinach Lasagne

1 pound spinach,
  cleaned
½ cup chopped onion
1 garlic clove,
  chopped
3 tablespoons butter
3 tablespoons flour
1½ cups light cream
2 cups ricotta cheese

½ cup freshly grated
  Parmesan cheese
¼ cup chopped flat-leaf
  parsley
2 eggs, beaten
9 lasagne noodles,
  cooked
2 cups grated
  mozzarella cheese

1. Cook the spinach until tender in water that clings to it; drain well and chop.
2. In a 1-quart saucepan, cook the onion and garlic in the butter until tender. Stir in the flour.
3. Gradually add the cream. Cook, stirring, for 3 minutes or until thickened; add the spinach.
4. Combine the ricotta and Parmesan cheeses, parsley, and eggs; mix well.
5. Lightly grease a 12- by 8-inch casserole. Arrange 3 lasagne noodles in the bottom of the casserole, trimming to fit. Top with one third of the spinach mixture, one third of the cheese mixture, and ½ cup mozzarella cheese. Repeat the layers twice more, ending with 1 cup mozzarella.
6. Bake in a 350-degree oven for 30 minutes. Let stand 15 minutes before serving. Serves 8.

Quick Penne Bake

1½ cups heavy cream
  2 tablespoons butter
    Salt and fresh
    pepper to taste
½ pound penne, cooked
  by method on pages
  92–3.

½ cup freshly grated
  Parmesan cheese

1. Heat the cream and butter in a saucepan until the butter melts. Add the salt and pepper.
2. Place the cooked penne in a shallow 9-inch baking dish. Pour the cream over. Add the cheese and toss. Bake in a 350-degree oven for 10–15 minutes until the cheese melts. Serves 4–6.

Macaroni and Cheese

This was the only pasta I knew as a kid. I had a racy aunt who made tomato sauce and spaghetti and meatballs, but my mother never attempted anything so un-American. You do see macaroni and cheese in Italy, but never in a casserole. Still, this is a homey, comfortable old dish, and good to eat.

½ pound small
  macaroni
  4 tablespoons butter
  1 small onion,
    chopped
½ cup dry white wine
  4 tablespoons flour
2½ cups light cream
½ cup cubed Bel Paese
  cheese

½ cup cubed Fontina
  cheese
  Salt and fresh pepper
  to taste
  Freshly grated
  nutmeg
  1 cup freshly grated
  Parmesan cheese

1. Cook the macaroni according to method on pages 92–3.
2. Heat the butter in a medium saucepan. When the foam subsides, add the onion. Stir with a wooden spatula until the onion wilts, about 3 minutes.
3. Add the wine and cook until it evaporates.
4. Add the flour and stir until well blended with the butter. Cook 3 minutes.
5. Add the cream and whisk until smooth.
6. Add the Bel Paese and Fontina and cook, stirring, until cheese melts. Season with salt, pepper, and nutmeg.
7. Place the cooked macaroni into a shallow 2-quart baking dish. Pour the sauce over and mix to combine. Sprinkle the top with Parmesan cheese. Serve as is or place in a 375-degree oven for 20 minutes, until bubbly and brown on top. Serves 6–8.

Pasta Pie

This recipe was given to me by Gino Hoppy, a friend from Kansas City.

½ pound spaghetti, cooked according to method on pages 92–3
4 tablespoons butter, melted
3 eggs, beaten
2 tablespoons oil
1 pound ground beef, veal, and pork, mixed
1 onion, chopped
1 garlic clove, chopped
1 small green pepper, seeded, filaments removed, and chopped

1½ pounds ripe tomatoes, peeled and chopped
Salt and fresh pepper
1 cup ricotta cheese
½ cup diced mozzarella cheese

1. In a large bowl, combine the pasta, butter, and eggs. Line a 10-inch pie plate with this mixture.
2. Heat the oil in a skillet. Add the meat and brown well for 3–4 minutes.
3. Add the onion, garlic, and green pepper. Cook another 3–4 minutes, stirring occasionally.
4. Add the tomatoes, salt, and pepper. Continue to cook 10 minutes longer. Drain off any excess fat.
5. Spread the ricotta cheese over the pasta mixture. Add the meat and top with the mozzarella. Bake at 350 degrees for 25 minutes. Serves 6.

Pasta Ring Mold

½ pound macaroni or broken noodles
1½ cups milk
1 cup fresh bread crumbs
6 tablespoons butter

½ pound freshly grated Parmesan cheese
3 eggs, beaten
Salt and fresh pepper to taste

1. Cook the pasta according to directions on pages 92–3.
2. While the pasta is cooking, prepare the sauce. Bring the milk to a boil. Lower the heat and add the bread crumbs. Stir with a whisk and beat in 4 tablespoons of the butter and the cheese. Carefully beat in the eggs. Whisk over low heat until smooth. Add salt and pepper.
3. Drain the pasta and place in a bowl. Add the remaining 2 tablespoons butter and toss. Add the cheese sauce and combine well. Fill a greased 6-cup ring mold with the mixture. Place in a water bath and bake 30 minutes in a 375-degree oven. Cook longer to set, if necessary. Let stand 5 minutes before unmolding onto a round platter. Serves 6.

Crespelle Luciano

Luciano Parolari, chef at the beautiful Villa d'Este hotel
in Lake Como, taught this recipe at my school several
years ago.

1¼ cups milk
   3 tablespoons butter
    Salt and fresh
    pepper to taste
    Freshly grated
    nutmeg to taste
¾ cup flour
   1 cup grated Gruyère
   cheese

   3 eggs, separated
6–8 crêpes (see
    following recipe)
    Thin béchamel
    sauce (see page 102)
    or 1½ cups heavy
    cream
½ cup freshly grated
    Parmesan cheese

1. Bring the milk to a boil. Add the butter, salt, pepper,
   and nutmeg. When the butter melts, add the flour all
   at one time. Beat with a wooden spatula over moderate
   heat until it forms a ball and comes away from the
   sides of the pan, as for cream puff pastry.
2. Put the mixture in a bowl. Add the Gruyère cheese.
   Beat well. The cheese will melt in the heat of the paste.
3. Add the egg yolks, one at a time. Beat them into the
   mixture and continue to beat until ingredients are
   incorporated.
4. Beat the egg whites until stiff but not dry. Fold into
   the paste mixture.
5. Lay the crêpes second side up. Place the paste mixture
   in a large pastry bag with tube opening the size of a
   dime. Pipe the mixture onto the crêpes, or spoon it
   on. Roll the crêpes to close.
6. Butter a baking dish and cover the bottom with one
   half the béchamel sauce, or heavy cream reduced to
   1 cup. Arrange the crêpes seam side down over the
   sauce. Spoon over the remainder of the béchamel sauce.
   Sprinkle with Parmesan cheese and bake in a 375-degree
   oven 30 minutes. Serves 6–8.

Variations

Crespelle roll. Spread the crêpe batter on a well-seasoned baking sheet. Bake in a 400-degree oven for 3 minutes. Remove and spread with filling. Roll into a long roll from the wide side, as for a jelly roll. Bake as above with béchamel and cheese.

Layered crespelle. The crêpes can be layered in a buttered dish just about the same size as the crêpes. Layer the crêpes, alternating béchamel, crêpe, cheese mixture, and ending with crêpe, béchamel, and Parmesan cheese. Bake as above.

Basic Crêpes

You can use crêpes instead of pasta in the lasagne and cannelloni recipes.

½ cup lightly spooned flour
2 eggs
2 egg yolks

¼ cup vegetable oil, plus oil to film crêpe pan
½ cup milk

1. Blend all the ingredients, except oil to film the pan, in a blender or food processor, or whisk in a bowl until smooth. Strain. Thin the batter, if necessary, with a little water or milk. It should be the consistency of heavy cream.
2. Heat a seasoned crêpe pan. Film the pan with oil and wipe out most of it. Add 2–3 tablespoons crêpe batter. Tilt and swirl the pan in all directions to spread the batter over the bottom of the pan. The crêpe should be very thin. Fry one side 1 minute. When the edges begin to pull away, turn over and fry the other side 30 seconds. Oil the pan as necessary between each crêpe. Makes 8 7-inch crêpes or 12 5-inch crêpes.

Béchamel Sauce

THIN

1 tablespoon butter
1 tablespoon flour
1 cup light cream
    Salt and fresh pepper
    to taste

MEDIUM

2 tablespoons butter
2 tablespoons flour
1 cup milk or cream

RICH

3 tablespoons butter
3 tablespoons flour
1 cup milk or cream

1. Melt the butter in a small saucepan. Don't let it brown.
2. Add the flour and stir with a wooden spatula, moving
   the mixture all around the bottom of the pan. Let the
   mixture bubble and foam, while stirring, for 3 minutes.
3. Add the cream or milk and switch to a whisk. Whisk
   until it thickens. Cook over very low heat for 15 minutes.
4. Season with salt and pepper. Makes about 1 cup.

Tomato Sauce I

4 pounds plum tomatoes
2 tablespoons butter
2 tablespoons oil
1 onion, finely chopped
2 large garlic cloves,
    chopped, or more to
    taste
    Tiny pinch of sugar
    (not much, but do
    use more sugar
    than salt here)

Salt and fresh
    pepper to taste
4–6 fresh basil leaves,
    finely chopped
¼ cup chicken stock
    (optional)

1. Slice off the tips of the tomatoes. Drop the tomatoes into boiling water for 10 seconds, then plunge into cold water with ice cubes. Squeeze each tomato in your hand and the skin will slip off in one piece. Finely chop the tomatoes.
2. Heat the butter and oil in a nonaluminum saucepan. Add the tomatoes and remaining ingredients and simmer until the sauce gives up most of its liquid and thickens, about 25 minutes. Serves 4–6.

Variation

Tomato cream sauce. Add ½ to 1 cup heavy cream to the finished sauce. For low-calorie sauce, eliminate the butter and oil.

Tomato Sauce II

4 tablespoons butter
1 large onion, chopped
1 carrot, chopped
2 celery ribs, chopped
2 garlic cloves, chopped
6–8 large tomatoes,
    peeled, seeded, and
    chopped

Salt and fresh black pepper
Pinch sugar
Few basil leaves

1. Melt the butter in a skillet. When the foam subsides, add the onion, carrot, celery, and garlic. Cook, while stirring with a wooden spoon, for 10 minutes.
2. Add the remaining ingredients and cook 20–25 minutes.
3. Purée the mixture through a food mill, using the fine blade. Makes 2–3 cups.

Raw Tomato Sauce

In the summer, when the tomatoes are at their peak, nothing surpasses this delightful sauce.

6–8 ripe tomatoes,
 peeled, seeded, and
 chopped
 12 basil leaves,
 chopped
 Salt and fresh
 pepper to taste
 ½ cup olive oil

1 pound spaghettini or
 bucatini, cooked
 according to method
 on pages 92–3
 Freshly grated
 Parmesan cheese to
 taste

Put the chopped tomatoes in a bowl. Add the chopped basil, salt, and pepper. Add the olive oil and mix well. Let stand at room temperature 15 minutes. Serve over hot cooked pasta. Toss and add cheese. Serves 4.

Large-Quantity Tomato Sauce

¼ cup olive oil
 1 very large onion,
 chopped
 2 garlic cloves, chopped
 8 pounds plum
 tomatoes, quartered

6 basil leaves, chopped
 Salt and fresh pepper
 to taste
 Pinch sugar, if
 necessary

1. Heat the oil in a very large kettle. Add the onion and garlic. Stir around for 2–3 minutes.
2. Add the tomatoes, basil, salt, pepper, and sugar. Cook down until excess liquid evaporates. This may take longer than the usual 25–30 minutes because of the quantity of tomatoes.

3. When thick, put through food mill, using the coarse
   blade. Makes 12 cups.

Note: This sauce freezes well, so make a lot and have it
for the winter.

Bolognese or Meat Sauce

4 tablespoons butter	1 cup dry red or white wine
1 large onion, chopped	2 or 3 very ripe tomatoes, peeled, seeded, and chopped
1 carrot, chopped	
1 celery rib, chopped	¾ cup chicken stock
1 garlic clove, chopped	Salt and fresh pepper
1½ pounds ground beef, veal, and pork, combined	3 or 4 chicken livers (optional)
	½ cup heavy cream

1. Melt 3 tablespoons of the butter in a large sauté pan.
   Add the onion, carrot, celery, and garlic. Cook, while
   stirring, on medium heat for 3–4 minutes.
2. Add the meat and raise the heat. Stir the meat until it
   is no longer pink, but don't brown it.
3. Add the wine, tomatoes, and chicken stock. Season
   with salt and pepper to taste. Partially cover the pan
   and cook on medium heat for ¾ to 1 hour.
4. Sauté the chicken livers in the remaining butter until
   crisp. Chop and add to the sauce.
5. Add the heavy cream, reheat, and serve over spaghetti,
   macaroni, penne or lasagna. Enough for 1½ pounds
   pasta.

Ricotta Cheese Sauce

1 cup ricotta cheese
1 cup heavy cream
¾ cup freshly grated
    Parmesan cheese
½ cup chopped
    prosciutto
    Salt and fresh pepper
    to taste

2 tablespoons chopped
    flat-leaf parsley
1 pound penne or shells,
    cooked by method on
    pages 92–3

In a large bowl, mix together the ricotta cheese, cream, Parmesan cheese, and prosciutto. Add salt, pepper, and parsley. Add the drained pasta and toss. Serves 4–6.

Gorgonzola Sauce I

This is Joel Kaye's recipe for gorgonzola sauce.

1½ cups heavy cream
½ pound Gorgonzola
    cheese, cut up
3 eggs, beaten

1 pound fettucine,
    cooked by method on
    pages 92–3

1. Place the cream and Gorgonzola cheese in a saucepan. Cook over low heat until the cheese melts. Let cook to reduce the cream for 3 or 4 minutes.
2. Temper the beaten eggs with a little hot sauce. Add the eggs to the sauce, whisk for 1 minute, and pour over hot pasta. Toss. Serves 4–6.

Gorgonzola Sauce II

1½ cups heavy cream
¼ pound Gorgonzola
  cheese, crumbled
1 pound wide noodles
  cooked by method on
  pages 92–3

Parmesan cheese

Bring the cream just to a boil. Add the Gorgonzola,
turn heat to low, and stir to melt. Pour over drained pasta.
Serve with freshly grated Parmesan cheese. Makes 4–6
servings.

Four Cheese Sauce

8 tablespoons butter
1 cup heavy cream
½ cup crumbled
  Gorgonzola cheese
½ cup shredded Gruyère
  cheese
½ cup cubed Fontina
  cheese

½ cup cubed mozzarella
1 pound tagliatelle,
  cooked by method on
  pages 92–3
Fresh pepper

1. Heat together the butter and cream.
2. Whisk in the cheeses, one at a time, until cheeses melt
   and a smooth sauce forms. If sauce is not fluid enough
   to pour, thin with more cream.
3. Pour over drained hot pasta. Season with freshly ground
   pepper. Toss and serve. Serves 4–6.

Carbonara Sauce

This is my favorite of all the carbonara sauces for pasta.
I adapted this from Nika Hazelton, author of *The Regional
Italian Kitchen*.

2 tablespoons butter
6 slices very lean
  bacon, cut into fine
  dice
1 small onion, chopped
⅔ cup dry white wine
3 eggs
4 tablespoons chopped
  flat-leaf parsley

Salt and fresh pepper
  to taste
⅔ cup freshly grated
  Parmesan cheese
1 pound spaghetti,
  cooked by method on
  pages 92–3

1. Melt the butter. When hot, add the bacon. Stir with a
   wooden spatula and cook for 3 minutes. Remove bacon
   to drain.
2. Add the onion and cook until onion is soft, about 5
   minutes.
3. Pour on the wine and stir until the wine has evaporated.
   Set aside but keep warm.
4. In a deep serving dish, beat together the eggs with the
   parsley, salt, Parmesan, and plenty of pepper. Add
   reserved bacon and onion mixture. Toss with hot pasta
   and mix well. Add the bacon and toss again. Serves
   4–6.

Gremolata Sauce

Gremolata is classically a mixture of parsley, lemon rind,
and garlic, usually served on osso buco. I had this sauce
one time with a faint mint taste that made it even better.
The secret is to make sure that the parsley and mint are

chopped very very fine—almost like green sawdust. What was once a garnish now becomes a sauce, and it tastes wonderful on pasta.

Grated peel and juice
of 1 lemon
2 garlic cloves, finely
chopped
1 tablespoon very finely
chopped mint
4 tablespoons very
finely chopped flat-
leaf parsley

1 pound linguine or
spaghettini, cooked
by method on
pages 92–3
½ cup olive oil

1. Place the grated lemon peel and garlic in a bowl. Add the mint, parsley, and lemon juice. Mix.
2. Toss the drained pasta with the oil. Add the parsley mixture, toss, and serve. Serves 4–6.

Parsley Butter Sauce

½ cup chopped flat-leaf
parsley
12 tablespoons butter,
melted
1 pound linguine,
cooked by method on
pages 92–3

¾ cup freshly grated
Parmesan cheese

In a small pan, heat the parsley with the melted butter. Pour over cooked pasta and toss with cheese. Serves 4–6.

Red Clam Sauce

4 tablespoons olive oil
1 garlic clove, chopped
1 onion, chopped
4 tomatoes, peeled,
  seeded, and chopped
2 tablespoons chopped
  flat-leaf parsley
Few basil leaves,
  chopped

1 teaspoon chopped
  oregano
3 dozen littleneck clams,
  shucked, with juice
1 pound linguine, cooked
  by method on
  pages 92–3

1. Heat the oil in a sauté pan. Add the garlic and onion and cook 3 minutes, stirring with a wooden spatula.
2. Add the tomatoes, parsley, basil, and oregano. Cook 5 minutes, stirring.
3. Add the clam juice. Bring to a boil and add the clams. Simmer 2 minutes and serve on hot pasta. Serves 4–6.

White Clam Sauce

6 tablespoons olive oil
3 garlic cloves, chopped
1 onion, chopped
2 tablespoons chopped
  flat-leaf parsley
4 tablespoons dry white
  wine

3 dozen littleneck clams,
  shucked, with juice
Salt and fresh pepper
  to taste
1 pound linguine, cooked
  by method on
  pages 92–3

1. Heat the oil in a large pan. Add the garlic and onion and cook 3 minutes, stirring with a wooden spatula.
2. Add the parsley, white wine, and juice from the clams. Bring to a boil. Reduce the heat and add the clams. Cook 2 minutes.
3. Season with salt and pepper and serve over pasta. Serves 4–6.

Butter and Marjoram Sauce

8 tablespoons butter
2 tablespoons chopped
   pine nuts, toasted (see
   note)
1 tablespoon chopped
   fresh marjoram
1 pound spaghetti,
   cooked by method on
   pages 92–3

Salt and fresh pepper
   to taste
1 cup freshly grated
   Parmesan cheese

1. Melt the butter in a small pan. Add the nuts and marjoram and cook 2–3 minutes.
2. Pour the sauce over the pasta and toss. Add salt and fresh pepper to taste. Sprinkle with cheese. Serves 4–6.

Note: To toast pine nuts, lay them on a baking sheet. Bake at 350 degrees for 10 minutes.

Creamy Mushroom Sauce

¼ cup butter
2 medium onions, thinly
   sliced
¼ pound thinly sliced
   prosciutto, cut into
   strips
½ pound fresh
   mushrooms, sliced
1 cup cooked peas

1½ cups heavy cream
¼ cup freshly grated
   Parmesan cheese
1 pound farfalle or
   bow-tie pasta,
   cooked by method
   on pages 92–3
Salt and fresh
   pepper to taste

1. Melt the butter in a large skillet. When the foam subsides, add the onions, prosciutto, and mushrooms and

cook until the vegetables are tender and all liquid from the mushrooms has evaporated.
2. Stir in the peas, cream, and cheese; heat through.
3. Pour the sauce over the hot pasta and toss to coat evenly. Season with salt and pepper. Serve with additional cheese, if desired. Serves 6.

Double Mushroom Sauce

2 ounces dried mushrooms, soaked in hot water to cover for 15 minutes
6 tablespoons butter
1 pound fresh mushrooms, cleaned and sliced

1 cup heavy cream
½ cup freshly grated Parmesan cheese
Salt and fresh pepper to taste
1 pound pappardelle cooked by method on pages 92–3

1. Drain the dried mushrooms, reserving ¼ cup of the liquid. Chop the mushrooms.
2. Melt the butter and add the dried and fresh mushrooms. Cook 3 minutes.
3. Add the cream, mushroom water, and cheese. Stir to mix well. Season with salt and pepper. Pour over pasta and toss. Serves 4.

Fresh Mushroom Sauce

5 tablespoons olive oil
1 pound mushrooms, sliced
Salt and fresh pepper to taste
Juice of 1 lemon
1 cup heavy cream

1 pound fettuccine, cooked by method on pages 92–3
6 tablespoons butter, melted
½ cup freshly grated Parmesan cheese

1. Heat the oil in a skillet. Add the mushrooms, salt, and pepper, and lemon juice. Toss over a high flame 3 minutes only.
2. Heat the heavy cream in a small pan.
3. Dress the pasta with the cream, butter, and cheese. Add the mushrooms and toss. Serves 4.

Mushroom and Garlic Sauce

8 tablespoons olive oil
2 garlic cloves, chopped
½ pound fresh mushrooms, cleaned and sliced
2 anchovies, drained and chopped

2 tablespoons chopped flat-leaf parsley
Salt and fresh pepper to taste
1 pound green spaghettini, cooked by method on pages 92–3

1. Heat the oil in a pan. When hot, add the garlic. Stir with a wooden spatula for 1 minute.
2. Add the mushrooms and anchovies. Cook, while stirring, 3 minutes.
3. Add the parsley and cook 1 minute longer. Add salt and pepper to taste and toss with the hot pasta. Serves 4–6.

Pesto

1½ cups fresh basil leaves
¾ cup olive oil
4 tablespoons soft butter
¼ cup pine nuts
¾ cup freshly grated Parmesan cheese

2 tablespoons chopped flat-leaf parsley
2 garlic cloves, chopped
Salt and fresh pepper to taste
1 pound trenette, cooked by method on pages 92–3

1. Put all the ingredients except salt, pepper, and pasta in a food blender and purée. (If using a blender, blend on low and then increase speed until mixture is puréed.) Season with salt and pepper.
2. Thin the sauce with 6 tablespoons water in which the pasta was cooked or warm water from the tap. Serve over pasta. Serves 4–6.

Serving Suggestions

Serve in soup without diluting with water.

Serve over tomatoes for salad.

Serve over boiled potatoes.

Serve over boiled potatoes and green beans.

Serve over gnocchi.

Leonardo's Sauce

8 tablespoons butter
1 cup chopped cooked ham
2 red peppers, seeded, filaments removed, and chopped
2 cups fresh peas
2 cups heavy cream

Salt and fresh pepper to taste
1 pound small rigatoni or penne, cooked by method on pages 92–3
¾ cup freshly grated Parmesan cheese

1. Melt the butter in a saucepan. Add the ham and sauté until crisp, about 3 minutes.
2. Add the peppers and cook, while stirring with a wooden spatula, 5 minutes more.

3. Add the peas, cream, salt, and pepper. Let come to a boil. Turn to a simmer and cook until the cream coats a spoon, 5–6 minutes. Serve over hot pasta. Toss with Parmesan cheese. Serves 4–6.

Primavera Sauce

This American invention is usually served over angel hair pasta, which I loathe. I much prefer to serve it over spaghettini. Notice the absence of broccoli and cauliflower, usually seen in this dish. For me they do not evoke springtime.

6 tablespoons olive oil
2 carrots, diced
2 zucchini, diced
4 tomatoes, peeled, seeded, and diced
1 small onion, chopped
1 clove garlic, chopped
1 or 2 peppers, red or green, chopped
½ cup chopped mushrooms
¼ cup chicken stock
2 or 3 basil leaves
½ pound green beans, diced
2 stalks asparagus, diced
1 cup heavy cream
Salt and fresh pepper
1 pound spaghettini, cooked by method on pages 92–3

1. Heat the olive oil in a large skillet. Add the carrots, zucchini, tomatoes, onion, garlic, peppers, and mushrooms. Cook, while stirring with a wooden spatula, for 5 minutes, or until the vegetables are barely tender.
2. Add the chicken stock and basil and cook until it is reduced.
3. Add the beans, asparagus, cream, salt, and pepper. Add a bit more stock, if the mixture seems too dry. Cook to heat the cream. Pour the mixture over hot pasta. Serves 4–6.

Broccoli and Goat Cheese Sauce

My Italian friends would cringe at the thought of this sauce made popular in California.

1 bunch broccoli
4 tablespoons olive oil
4 tablespoons butter
¼ pound soft goat
  cheese
Salt and fresh pepper
  to taste

1½ cups chicken stock
1 pound green
  spaghettini, cooked
  by method on pages
  92–3

1. Trim the broccoli. Separate into flowerets. Reserve the stems for another use.
2. Heat the oil in a skillet. When hot, add the broccoli and stir-fry until barely tender, 3–5 minutes.
3. Add the butter, goat cheese, salt, and pepper. Stir until the cheese melts.
4. Add the stock. Cook uncovered until the flavors blend, 3–5 minutes.
5. Pour over hot pasta and toss. Serves 4–6.

Anchovy Sauce

¼ cup olive oil
1 can (2 ounces)
  anchovies, drained
  and chopped
2 garlic cloves, chopped
2 cups tomato sauce I
  or II (see pages 102–103)
¼ cup chopped flat-leaf
  parsley
¼ cup pitted, chopped
  black olives

2 tablespoons capers,
  drained
1 pound spaghetti or
  linguine, cooked by
  method on pages 92–3
½ cup freshly grated
  Parmesan cheese
  (optional)

1. Heat the oil in a saucepan. Add the anchovies and garlic. Cook until the anchovies melt, about 5 minutes.
2. Add the tomato sauce and parsley. Simmer 5 minutes.
3. Add the olives and capers. Simmer 12 minutes, stirring frequently. Serve over pasta, with grated cheese, if desired. Serves 4–6.

Note: This sauce is also good over grilled fish.

Prosciutto, Spinach, and Cream Sauce

3 cups heavy cream
3 tablespoons butter
¼ pound prosciutto, diced
1½ cups shredded spinach
Salt and fresh pepper to taste

½ cup freshly grated Parmesan cheese
1 pound small seashell pasta, cooked by method on pages 92–3

1. Reduce the cream over medium heat to 1½ cups.
2. Heat the butter in a large skillet. Sauté the ham for 1 minute. Add the cream and spinach and cook until the mixture coats a spoon.
3. Season with salt and pepper and toss with the cheese over hot pasta. Serves 4–6.

Spinach-Cheese Sauce

1 pound fresh spinach, washed and stems removed
2 tablespoons butter
½ cup ricotta cheese
¼ cup freshly grated Parmesan cheese
Salt and pepper to taste

Grated nutmeg to taste
1¼ cups heavy cream
1 pound orecchiette (little ears), cooked by method on pages 92–3

1. Cook the spinach in a large saucepan with water that clings to it until wilted; drain.
2. Squeeze well to remove as much moisture as possible; chop finely.
3. In a large skillet, sauté the chopped spinach in butter.
4. Stir in the remaining ingredients except pasta, and heat but do not boil. Serve with pasta. Serves 4–6.

Spinach and Cream Sauce

2 cups heavy cream
2 tablespoons butter
¼ pound thinly sliced
    prosciutto, chopped
8 ounces fresh spinach
Salt and fresh pepper
    to taste

1 pound trenette or
    spaghetti, cooked by
    method on pages 92–3
½ cup freshly grated
    Parmesan cheese

1. Put the cream in a small saucepan and bring to a boil. Reduce to 1½ cups.
2. Heat the butter in a sauté pan and, when foam subsides, add the ham. Cook, while stirring, 2 minutes.
3. Stem and wash and dry the spinach. Cut in julienne strips.
4. Combine the cream and ham and add the spinach. Cook 3 minutes. Season with salt and pepper. Pour over pasta and sprinkle with cheese. Toss. Serves 4–6.

Lemon Sauce

Delicate but very very good.

Zest of 1 lemon
1½ cups heavy cream
Juice of ½ lemon
2 tablespoons chopped
    flat-leaf parsley
Grated fresh nutmeg
    to taste

Salt and fresh pepper
    to taste
1 pound spaghetti,
    cooked by method on
    pages 92–3

1. Put the lemon zest and cream in a small pan and let steep for 10 minutes over very low heat.
2. Stir in the lemon juice, parsley, and nutmeg. Season with salt and pepper. Whisk until hot and pour over hot pasta. Serves 4–6.

Fettuccine with Shrimp and Fresh Peas

1½ pounds shrimp, peeled and deveined, shells reserved
1 pound peas, shelled
1 small onion, finely chopped
½ cup sliced mushrooms
¼ cup dry vermouth
2 cups heavy cream
Salt and fresh pepper to taste
1 pound spinach fettuccine, cooked by method on pages 92–3

1. Place the shrimp shells in water to cover. Bring to a boil. Cover and cook on moderate heat 20 minutes. Strain. Reserve 1½ cups of stock.
2. Place the peas in a saucepan with just enough water to cover. Bring to a boil, reduce heat to moderate, and cook 10 minutes, or until barely tender.
3. Add the shrimp to the peas (it may be necessary to add more water but do not add too much). Cook until the shrimp are just poached, 2–3 minutes. Strain and reserve the juices. Place the shrimp and peas back in the pan.
4. In another saucepan, place the onion, mushrooms, dry vermouth, reserved shrimp stock, and strained juices from shrimp and peas. Reduce over moderate heat to approximately 1 cup.
5. Add the heavy cream and cook until the mixture coats the back of a metal spoon.
6. Combine the reduced mixture with the peas and shrimp. Reheat. Season with salt and pepper to taste. Serve over hot pasta. Serves 4–6.

Fettuccine Alfredo

One of the most popular pasta dishes ever to come out of Italy.

8 tablespoons butter, softened
¾ cup freshly grated Parmesan cheese
¼ cup heavy cream

Salt and fresh pepper to taste
1 pound fettuccine, cooked by method on pages 92–3

1. Place the butter in a bowl and beat with a wooden spatula until soft.
2. Add the cheese and combine. Add the heavy cream and mix well. Season with salt and pepper. Toss with hot fettuccine. Serves 4–6.

Fettuccine and Cabbage

4 tablespoons butter
1 head (1½ pounds) cabbage, coarsely sliced
1 large onion, thinly sliced
½ teaspoon fennel seed
2 cups light cream

Salt and fresh pepper to taste
1 pound fettuccine, cooked according to method on pages 92–3
½ cup freshly grated Parmesan cheese

1. Melt the butter in a large skillet. Cook the cabbage, onion, and fennel in the butter a few minutes. Reduce the heat to low, cover, and cook until the cabbage is tender, stirring occasionally, about 15 minutes. Add the cream, salt, and pepper to the cabbage; heat through.
2. Pour the cabbage over the cooked pasta and toss with cheese. Serves 6.

Zucchini and Linguine

4 medium zucchini
¼ cup olive oil
2 garlic cloves, chopped
Salt and fresh pepper
to taste

1 pound linguine, cooked
by method on pages
92–3
Freshly grated
Parmesan cheese

1. Wash and dry the zucchini. Remove the ends. Using the julienne blade on a mandoline, cut the zucchini into very long shreds.
2. Heat the oil in a sauté pan. Add the garlic and stir for 1–2 minutes. Add the zucchini and toss for 4–5 minutes over high heat.
3. Season with salt and pepper and toss with hot linguine. Sprinkle with cheese. Serves 4–6.

6

RICE, GNOCCHI AND POLENTA

IN ITALY, THE ONLY TIME RICE IS SERVED WITH A MAIN course is when risotto Milanese is served with osso buco. Otherwise, rice is the main course or the pasta course.

Risotto is made with rice, good stock, a little care in cooking, and almost any other ingredient you can think of. It is a perfect one-course meal, and I always make sure to keep a few bags or boxes of Italian rice on hand as an emergency food. Just unfreeze a quart of stock and break out the leftovers; you'll make something delicious out of it.

Italian rice, especially from the Po Valley in Piedmont, makes the best risotto—it is short-grained and absorbent, and gives you a risotto that is creamy and moist, with every grain still separate. You can make risotto with American rice, if you have to, but look around for the Italian brands; they're getting easier and easier to find. Among the best I know are: Arborio, Superfino, and Carnoroli (hardest to find in the States).

Italians do not use cheese in seafood risottos. Try it

the traditional way first, and see if you don't like it.

Leftover risotto, if you ever have such a thing, is not a problem. In Milan, they make a rice cake out of it—there's a special little iron skillet in which the risotto is fried a dark and crusty brown first on one side then on the other before being cut into wedges and served. Or risotto can be wrapped into a ball around a bit of cheese, breaded, and fried a golden brown.

Whichever way you flavor your risottos, and whatever you do with the leftovers, this is a simple and basic recipe based on a simple and basic idea—stock is added to sautéed rice in small amounts so that the rice absorbs all the liquid. Of course stirring helps this, of course you don't want to lose all the stock and scorch the rice, and of course risotto tastes best when it is served as soon as it is done.

But making risotto is not martyrdom. You don't have to agonize over it. If you're in the middle of making it and you want to walk across a room to dress a salad or answer the phone—go ahead. As long as the rice doesn't burn, the risotto will taste fine anyway. And if you have to hold risotto for some late dinner guest, or because you misjudged the timing of something else you're having for dinner, go ahead and do that, too. Food is meant to please people, not to frighten them.

Gnocchi can be made of potato, or potato and flour, or semolina, spinach, cheese, or even meat. The ones I like best are rolled on the inside of a fork, or on a cheese grate or butter paddle to give them a series of nice little ridges. And the ones I like best are not heavy.

Polenta is a staple of Northern Italy, rarely seen south of Rome, although it is like the corn meal mush of our Southern states. It is usually made in a special copper pan, with a specially designed wooden spoon to stir the mush. I have one of these things somewhere around my kitchen, but I've never used it. Any good heavy pot and any wooden spoon will do.

In Italy, polenta is poured from its pot onto a big bread board; the wood is enough to keep it from slopping over too much and winding up on the floor. It is then allowed to cool and cut—with a string. I don't know why a string is used, a knife works just as well; but the string is traditional. Polenta is usually the bland accompaniment to a highly flavored meat, but occasionally it is served with a very rich tomato sauce. Or cheese is laid between two layers of polenta, sandwich fashion, the outside brushed with oil, and the polenta fried or run under the broiler to brown.

Risotto

Carlo Ciccarelli, chef of the Gritti Palace hotel in Venice, taught me a very long time ago how to make risotto. He stood over me time and time again until I got it just right.

5 cups, more or less, chicken stock
4 tablespoons butter
1 large onion, chopped
1 garlic clove, chopped
2 cups Italian rice
6 tablespoons dry white wine
Salt and fresh pepper to taste

½ teaspoon saffron threads (optional)
8 tablespoons butter, softened
2–4 tablespoons freshly grated Parmesan cheese

1. Bring the stock to a boil and hold at a simmer.
2. In a heavy-bottomed casserole, melt the 4 tablespoons butter. Add the onion and garlic. Cook over medium-high heat for a few minutes until the onion is limp.
3. Reduce the heat to a simmer and add the rice, stirring to coat the rice with butter.
4. Add the wine. Raise the heat and cook, stirring, until the wine is absorbed. Add salt and pepper.

5. Dissolve the saffron in a bit of stock and add.
6. Start adding the stock, a ladleful at a time. Stir with a wooden spatula to keep the rice from sticking. When the stock is absorbed, add another ladleful. Continue adding stock gradually until the rice is cooked. It should have a creamy consistency, but the rice should have a bite to it. The rice mixture should not be dry like a pilaf.
7. Remove the pan from the heat and add the softened butter and Parmesan cheese. Stir it gently. Serve immediately. Serves 6.

Variations

Seafood risotto. Omit the garlic, saffron, and Parmesan cheese. Sauté 2 cups of mixed seafood—lobster chunks, shrimp, clams, or mussels—in 2 tablespoons butter for 2–3 minutes. Flame with 3 tablespoons Cognac. Add to the risotto with the final addition of stock. Omit the cheese.

Risotto with sausage. Omit the saffron and wine. Remove the casings from ½ pound sweet or hot sausage. Break up and sauté sausage meat in 2 tablespoons olive oil until brown. Remove the sausage with a slotted spoon and add to the rice with the final addition of stock. Add 2 or 3 tablespoons soft butter and 2 tablespoons Parmesan cheese.

Risotto primavera. Omit the saffron. Dice 2 small zucchini, 1 small green or red pepper, 12 green beans, and ¼ pound mushrooms. Stir-fry or sauté the vegetables in 2–3 tablespoons oil or butter until barely tender. Add to the risotto mixture before the last addition of stock. Add the butter and Parmesan cheese.

Risotto with truffles. Omit the saffron. Add as many slivers or shavings of white truffle as desired just before serving the risotto.

Risotto with dried mushrooms. Omit the saffron. Soak 2 ounces dried porcini in warm water to cover for ½ hour. Drain and chop. Strain the soaking water through a hair sieve and reserve. Add the chopped porcini to the pan with the rice and stir. Add the mushroom water with the final addition of stock. Add the butter and Parmesan cheese.

Risotto with fresh asparagus tips. Omit the saffron and garlic. Steam or boil in water to cover the tips from 1 pound young asparagus until tender crisp, 2–3 minutes. Add to the risotto before the final addition of stock. The water from cooking or steaming the asparagus can be added to the stock for more flavor. Add butter and Parmesan cheese.

Risotto with peas. Omit the saffron and garlic. Cook 3 cups fresh peas until barely tender, 10–12 minutes. Remove ½ cup of peas and purée in a blender. Drain the remaining peas. Add the purée to the risotto when the rice is half cooked. Add the drained peas just before the final addition of stock. This risotto should be wetter than regular risotto. Add butter and Parmesan cheese.

Gnocchi Roman Style

1 quart milk	2 egg yolks
1 cup semolina or cream farina	Butter for greasing baking dish
¾ cup freshly grated Parmesan cheese Salt and fresh pepper to taste	6 tablespoons butter, melted
	½ cup freshly grated Parmesan cheese

1. Heat the milk to the boiling point.
2. Pour the semolina slowly in a thin stream into the milk.

Beat constantly with a wooden spatula until the mixture thickens, contains no lumps, and leaves the sides of the pan.

3. Remove from the heat and beat in ¾ cup Parmesan cheese, salt, pepper, and egg yolks.

4. Spread out on an oiled marble slab or countertop. Smooth the top with a wet spatula or an oiled rolling pin. Allow to cool for 15–20 minutes until the mixture sets. (To hasten cooling, spread the mixture on an oiled baking sheet and chill in the refrigerator.)

5. When the mixture sets, cut into 2-inch rounds, or cut free hand into diamond or square shapes. Place in buttered baking dish. Sprinkle with melted butter and ½ cup Parmesan cheese.

6. Bake at 375 degrees until brown on top, 10–15 minutes. Just before serving, glaze under the broiler for 1 minute. Serves 6.

Note: Place the gnocchi trimmings in the baking dish and overlap the rounds on top of them.

Variations

Sauté ¼ pound chopped prosciutto in 2 tablespoons butter and add to the gnocchi mixture.

Chop ½ fresh white truffle and add to the mixture.

Substitute water for milk.

Add 2 teaspoons strong mustard, ¼ cup Parmesan cheese, and 2 tablespoons melted butter to basic mixture.

Serve with thin béchamel sauce (page 102) spooned over and Parmesan cheese sprinkled on top.

Dust top of gnocchi with 4 tablespoons bread crumbs, butter, and Parmesan.

Serve with tomato sauce I or II (pages 102–103).

Serve with sage butter, made by melting 8 tablespoons butter with 3 or 4 fresh sage leaves in a pan until brown. Remove the sage leaves and pour the butter over the gnocchi.

Spinach Gnocchi

2 cups water
4 tablespoons butter
2 cups flour
1 cup raw spinach, washed, dried, stems removed, and puréed in a food processor
2 eggs
2 egg whites
Salt and fresh pepper to taste
Freshly grated nutmeg to taste
⅔ cup freshly grated Parmesan cheese
6 tablespoons butter, melted
½ cup freshly grated Parmesan cheese

1. Put the water in a pan with the 4 tablespoons butter and bring slowly to a boil.
2. Add the flour and spinach and stir over medium heat to combine.
3. Transfer to a mixing bowl and add the eggs and egg whites one at a time. Beat until shiny.
4. Add salt, pepper, nutmeg, and ⅔ cup of the cheese. Beat just to combine.
5. Fill a pastry bag fitted with a tube the size of a quarter with the mixture.
6. Bring a kettle of water to a boil (a wide pan is best). Lay the end of the pastry bag on the edge of the pan

and squeeze gently. As the mixture extrudes, cut it off every inch using a sharp knife. Let the pieces fall into the simmering water. Simmer very gently for 15 minutes, or until the gnocchi are cooked through.

7. Drain. Place them on a buttered, ovenproof serving dish. Dot with the 6 tablespoons butter and sprinkle with ½ cup Parmesan cheese. Bake at 375 degrees for 10–15 minutes, or until bubbly. Serves 6.

Variation

Mushroom gnocchi. Chop ¼ pound mushrooms very fine. Sauté until dry in 2 tablespoons butter and the juice of ½ lemon. Add to the gnocchi mixture instead of spinach.

Potato Gnocchi

These are delicious and delicate when made properly. There is nothing worse than a tough gnocchi dish.

1 pound old potatoes	*¼ cup flour, or more*
2 egg yolks	*6 tablespoons butter,*
Salt and fresh pepper	*melted*
to taste	*½ cup freshly grated*
Freshly grated nutmeg	*Parmesan cheese*
to taste	

1. Boil the potatoes in their skins until cooked through. Do not pierce unnecessarily while cooking. When soft, remove and peel while hot.
2. Return the potatoes to the pan and break up with a fork. Shake over a low flame to dry out completely. Put the potatoes through a ricer or beat until smooth in a mixer.
3. Beat in the yolks, salt, pepper, and nutmeg.

4. Add the flour, a little at a time. Use just enough flour to make the mixture manageable. If too much flour is used, the gnocchi will be hard as rocks. If too little flour is used, the mixture will fall apart. After making these a few times, you develop a feel for them.

5. On a floured board, form the mixture into rope shapes the width of your thumb. Keep the hands floured. Cut off the gnocchi every ¾ inch. Do not stack them. On the floured board, make indentations on each one with the tines of a fork, or roll each one down the inside of a fork, cheese grater, or butter paddle. They should look like little shells.

6. Drop a few at a time into a wide pan of simmering salted water. They will rise to the top. Cook 3 minutes and remove with a slotted spoon to a buttered baking dish.

7. Sprinkle the butter and cheese over the gnocchi and bake at 350 degrees for 15–20 minutes. Serve with tomato sauce, sage butter, or pesto. Serves 6.

Note: Sometimes I add 1 teaspoon baking powder to the gnocchi mixture.

Polenta

4 cups water	½ cup freshly grated
1 cup corn meal, yellow	Parmesan cheese
or white	4 tablespoons butter
Salt and fresh pepper	
to taste	

1. Bring the water to a boil in a medium-size saucepan. Turn to a simmer and add the corn meal in a thin stream. Beat with a wooden spoon continuously until all the corn meal is added. I find it easy to add the corn meal by placing it on wax paper and gathering

the paper together at one end to make a cone, letting the corn meal fall in the water slowly.

2. Beat on moderate heat until the mixture thickens and comes away from the sides of the pan. The fine corn meal found in the supermarkets will thicken in 15–20 minutes. Coarse, stone-ground corn meal will take 30–40 minutes.

3. When it thickens, add salt, pepper, Parmesan cheese, and butter. Beat until the cheese and butter are incorporated.

4. Pour onto a wooden board or platter and cut into individual portions. Serve in place of a starch with the main course. Or serve with fresh tomato or meat sauce. Serves 6–8.

Variations

Fried polenta. Cut the polenta into pieces and fry in oil or butter until crisp on both sides.

Broiled or grilled polenta. Brush pieces of polenta with olive oil and place on the broiler rack 2 inches from the heating element. Broil 1 minute on each side. Or place on a grill over charcoal, 4 to 6 inches, from gray coals. Grill 1 minute on each side.

Filled Polenta

2 tablespoons dry
  bread crumbs
  Cooked polenta (see
  page 130)
4 tablespoons butter
1½ cups sliced
  mushrooms
  Salt and fresh pepper
  to taste

Juice of ½ lemon
4 tablespoons freshly
  grated Parmesan
  cheese
6 tablespoons heavy
  cream

1. Butter a 9-inch baking dish and add the bread crumbs. Turn the dish so it is evenly coated. Place half the polenta in the dish.
2. Heat 2 tablespoons of the butter in a small skillet. When the foam subsides, add the mushrooms, salt, and pepper. Toss the mushrooms over high heat 2–3 minutes. Sprinkle the lemon juice over.
3. Place the mushrooms on the polenta. Sprinkle with the Parmesan cheese. Drizzle 4 tablespoons of the cream over and top with the rest of the polenta. Dot the top with the remaining butter and cream.
4. Bake in a 375-degree oven for 15–20 minutes. Cut into portions and serve hot. Serves 6–8.

Note: Any leftovers can be sliced and fried in butter or oil.

7

PIZZA, EGGS AND SANDWICHES

"If you want to know what a pizza is take a piece of dough, roll it out, then pummel it a bit with the flat of your hands, cover it with anything at all, moisten it with oil or lard, bake it in the oven and eat it." That description from Massimo Alberini's *Pasta and Pizza* is the best I've ever seen. In Italy, pizzas are usually made in brick ovens, and are usually lighter than American pizzas—the crust is more delicate, the topping much more simple. I make pizza at home my own way. It is quick, easy, delicious— and I do not bother with oven tiles or commercial pizza stones.

Just make the pizza. The kids will love it.

My kids still love it when they come back home—from college, or for a vacation, or to bring along the fiancé to meet the family. Pizza helps everybody relax.

I've included other snacks and luncheon dishes in this chapter for adults as well as the kids.

Pizza

I never allow my pizza dough to rise until double. I let it rest for 30 minutes and go ahead with the pizza. I am not looking for a raised crust. I like it as thin as possible.

THE CRUST:

1 package active dry yeast
1 cup lukewarm water (110 degrees)
2 tablespoons olive oil
1 teaspoon salt
3 cups flour, approximately

TOPPINGS:

¼ pound cooked sliced mushrooms
¼ pound thinly sliced pepperoni or salami
½ pound cooked, drained Italian sausage
2 cans (2 ounces each) anchovy fillets, drained, and/or tuna fish
½ cup sliced pitted ripe or pimiento-stuffed olives
2 cups tomato sauce
2 cups mozzarella cheese or provolone
Few sprigs fresh oregano or basil
6 tablespoons freshly grated Parmesan cheese

1. In a small bowl, sprinkle the yeast over ¼ cup lukewarm water. Let stand 5 minutes to dissolve.
2. In a large bowl, combine the remaining ¾ cup water, oil, and salt. Stir in the dissolved yeast. Add the flour, 1 cup at a time, beating after each addition.
3. Turn the dough onto a lightly floured surface. Knead about 5 minutes, or until all the flour has been worked into the mixture. Let rest 30 minutes.

To assemble:
4. Preheat the oven to 450 degrees.
5. Brush a 12-inch pizza pan lightly with additional oil.

Roll the dough into a 14-inch circle. Place in the prepared pan and form a rim around the edge.

6. Spread 1 cup tomato sauce I or II (see pages 102–103) over the dough. Top with any of the toppings listed or a combination of your choice.

7. Sprinkle with 1 cup shredded mozzarella cheese. Drizzle a little oil over the pizza before and after baking. Bake 20–25 minutes until crust is browned and crisp. Serves 6.

Note: Cut the dough in half and make two smaller pizzas, 6–7 inches wide.

Variations

Add 1 large chopped onion sautéed in 2 tablespoons olive oil and put on top of the tomato sauce. Add cheese.

Add ground cooked meat.

Add sliced cooked artichoke hearts.

Add sautéed pepper strips.

Add hot peppers.

Add chopped garlic.

Add baby clams or mussels.

Add goat cheese slices and sun-dried tomatoes.

Calzone, Stromboli, or Panzarotti

A stromboli is anything rolled up in pizza dough. The calzone is folded over into a crescent shape. Panzarotti are small stuffed crescents, deep fried.

THE DOUGH:

2 packages active dry
yeast
1 cup warm water (110
degrees)

3 tablespoons olive oil
1 teaspoon salt
4 cups flour

THE FILLING:

2 tablespoons olive oil
6 cups sliced onions
1 cup pitted and roughly
chopped black olives
4 tomatoes, peeled,
seeded, and roughly
chopped
½ cup freshly grated
Parmesan cheese

½ cup grated mozzarella
cheese
1 small tin anchovies,
drained and chopped,
or use ham or
pepperoni

1. Place the yeast in ½ cup of the warm water. Stir to
   dissolve and let stand 4–5 minutes.
2. Put the olive oil, salt, and remaining ½ cup warm water
   in a mixer bowl. Add the yeast mixture. Add 1 cup
   flour and beat. Reduce the mixer speed to slow and
   add the remaining flour. When thoroughly mixed, turn
   the dough out onto a lightly floured counter.
3. Knead 5–6 minutes until smooth and elastic. Place in
   a bowl, cover loosely, and let stand 30 minutes.
4. Heat the oil in a large skillet. When hot, add the onions
   and cook gently until wilted.
5. Add the olives, anchovies, and tomatoes. Simmer 10
   minutes.
6. Add the Parmesan cheese. Stir well and allow to cool
   slightly. Just before placing on rolled out dough, add
   the mozzarella cheese.

For calzone: Divide the dough into 6–8 pieces. Lay
each piece on a floured board and roll into a circle. Place
some filling on the lower half of each circle. Brush the

edges with water and fold to form a half-moon shape. Let rise 15–20 minutes. Bake 30–35 minutes at 400 degrees. Serves 6–8.

For stromboli: Roll the dough on floured board into a 12- by 18-inch rectangle. Spread the filling on the dough, leaving a 1½-inch margin all around. Fold the short ends inward over the filling. Roll from the long side as for a jelly roll. Brush the edges with water to seal. Place on a lightly oiled baking dish. Cover. Let rise 30 minutes. Brush with olive oil. Bake 15 minutes at 400 degrees. Serves 6–8.

For panzarotti: Pinch off walnut-size pieces of dough. Roll each into a round. Fill each round with a piece of mozzarella cheese, a piece of basil leaf, a piece of tomato or a tiny bit of tomato sauce. Sprinkle with Pecorino cheese. Fold the edges together and pinch with the tines of a fork. Deep fry in hot fat. Serve hot. Serves 6–8.

Egg Pizza

4 tablespoon oil	¾ cup tomato sauce I
8 eggs	(see page 102)
3 tablespoons water	½ cup grated mozzarella
Salt and fresh pepper	cheese
to taste	¼ cup freshly grated
1 teaspoon oregano	Parmesan cheese

1. Heat the oil in a 8- or 10-inch skillet.
2. Beat the eggs with the water, salt, pepper, and oregano. Add to the skillet. Reduce heat. Allow the eggs to cook until the bottom is firm. Lift the edges, allowing uncooked mixture to run under. Cook until the top is nearly firm.
3. Spoon the tomato sauce over the eggs. Sprinkle with the cheeses and run under the broiler until bubbly and cheese is just melted. Serve in wedges. Serves 4–6.

Variations

2 tablespoons butter or oil	1 small red onion, peeled and thinly sliced
1 small green or red pepper, seeded and very thinly sliced	Salt and fresh pepper to taste

Anchovy topping. Lay anchovies from 1 small can, drained, over the egg pizza. Scatter the cheese on top. Broil.

Pepper and onion topping. Melt the butter in a small skillet. When hot, add the peppers, onion, salt, and pepper. Stir around until just wilted. Scatter over egg pizza, add the cheese, and run under the broiler until the cheese melts.

Frittata

Frittatas are a great luncheon dish, served hot or at room temperature. Or cut in wedges and serve with drinks or take along on a picnic. Almost anything can be added to a frittata—even left-over spaghetti. Here are a few ideas.

6 eggs	2 small zucchini, shredded on a mandoline or grater
Salt and fresh pepper to taste	
4 tablespoons oil	¼ cup freshly grated Parmesan cheese
2 tablespoons butter	

1. Break the eggs into a bowl. Add salt and pepper. Beat with a whisk until well mixed but not frothy.

2. Add the oil and butter to an 8-inch nonstick pan. When the oil is hot and the butter melted, add the eggs. Scatter the zucchini on top. Mix gently with the flat side of a fork. Cook on medium heat until mixture is set. Lift the edges occasionally to see if the bottom is brown. When the mixture is set, the frittata will slide in the pan but the top will be liquid.

3. Sprinkle the Parmesan cheese over the top and set under a very hot broiler for about 2 minutes, watching carefully. Slide onto a round dish and cut into wedges. Serves 4.

Note: Frittatas can be made with a handful of fresh spinach, some raw onion, or leftover cooked vegetables. You can also add some ham, cooked bacon, sausage, potatoes, or tomato.

Variations

Parmesan frittata. Add 1 cup freshly grated Parmesan cheese to the egg mixture. Cook as per basic recipe. Sprinkle the top with 2 tablespoons Parmesan and run under the broiler.

Artichoke frittata. Cut 3 very small artichokes in half, remove chokes, cut into pieces and sauté in 4 tablespoons hot oil. Add to eggs and cook as per basic recipe.

Tomato and basil frittata. Add 1 cup peeled, seeded, and chopped tomatoes along with 4 basil leaves, chopped, to the eggs.

Mushroom frittata. Sauté 1 cup sliced mushrooms in 2 tablespoons oil. Sprinkle on the juice of ½ lemon. Cook 3 minutes. Add to eggs.

Cauliflower or Broccoli with Fried Eggs

Cooked cauliflower or   Fresh pepper to
broccoli flowerets   taste
4 tablespoons butter,   4–6 tablespoons butter
melted   4–6 eggs
½ cup freshly grated
Parmesan cheese

1. Place the hot cooked vegetable in a baking dish. Drizzle 4 tablespoons butter over and sprinkle with cheese and pepper. Place in a 375-degree oven for 3 minutes.
2. Heat 1 tablespoon of butter for each egg and let it brown. Fry the eggs.
3. Remove the vegetable from the oven and place the fried eggs on top. Serves 4–6.

Note: This is also good with asparagus.

Eggs with Eggplant

¼ cup olive oil   Salt and fresh pepper
2 small eggplants, diced   to taste
1 medium onion,   6 eggs
chopped   6 tablespoons freshly
1 garlic clove, chopped   grated Parmesan
2 tomatoes, peeled,   cheese
seeded, and chopped

1. Heat the oil in a skillet. When hot, add the eggplant, onion, garlic, and tomatoes. Cook, stirring with a wooden spatula, for 10 minutes. Season with salt and pepper.
2. Place the mixture in each of six small casseroles. Break an egg on top of each. Place the casseroles on a baking sheet and bake in a 400-degree oven until the eggs are set, 5–7 minutes. Sprinkle with Parmesan cheese and serve. Serves 6.

Eggs Parmesan

8 eggs
1 tablespoon salt
Olive oil for frying
4 tablespoons flour

½ cup milk
1 cup freshly grated
Parmesan cheese

1. Put the eggs into a pan of cold water. Add salt. Bring to a boil and boil 12 minutes, turning the eggs over occasionally. Turn off heat. Let stand 5 minutes. Plunge the eggs into ice water to cool. Drain and peel.
2. Heat 2 inches of oil to 350–360 degrees.
3. Roll the peeled eggs in flour. Dip in milk. Roll in Parmesan cheese. Gently lower the eggs into the oil. Fry 30–35 seconds, turning to brown evenly. Do not overcook as cheese will burn. Drain on absorbent paper. Serves 4–6.

Note: Serve with tomato sauce as a lunch dish or eat as a snack.

Spinach and Prosciutto Custard

This is essentially a quiche without a crust. It makes an elegant first course, and an unusual and delicious main course for breakfast or brunch.

1 pound spinach,
washed and stems
removed
3 tablespoons butter
1 small onion, chopped
¼ pound prosciutto,
chopped
2 eggs

2 egg yolks
2 cups light cream
Salt and fresh pepper
to taste
Grated nutmeg to
taste
¼ cup toasted pine nuts
(optional)

1. Chop the spinach and place in a pan just with water clinging to it. Stir over medium heat to wilt. Put the

spinach in a towel and squeeze both ends to remove liquid. Place in a bowl.

2. Melt 2 tablespoons of the butter in a small skillet. Add the onion and cook 1–2 minutes, stirring. Add to the spinach.

3. In the same pan, melt the remaining tablespoon butter. When hot, add the prosciutto and cook 1–2 minutes. Add to the spinach mixture.

4. Whisk the eggs, egg yolks, and cream together. Combine with the spinach mixture. Add salt, pepper, nutmeg, and pine nuts. Gently pour the custard into a greased 9-by-1½-inch baking dish. Bake at 350 degrees for 20 minutes, or until the custard is set. A silver knife inserted in it will come out clean. Serves 6–8.

Prosciutto Soufflé

4 tablespoons butter	1 cup finely chopped
¼ cup finely chopped	prosciutto (¼ pound
onion	lean ham)
3 tablespoons flour	5 egg yolks
½ cup chicken stock	7 egg whites
½ cup light cream	
Salt and fresh pepper	
to taste	

1. Preheat the oven to 375 degrees with the oven rack at bottom shelf.

2. Have ready a 1½-quart soufflé dish. Do not grease the dish.

3. Melt the butter in a small saucepan. On high heat, sauté the onion and stir blend the flour.

4. Add the chicken stock and cream, whisking until the mixture thickens and is smooth and has come to a boil. Season with salt and pepper.

5. Remove from the heat and add the chopped prosciutto. Transfer the ham mixture to a large bowl to cool for 3–5 minutes.

6. Beat the egg yolks until light lemon color and thick. Fold the beaten yolks, a little at a time, into the ham mixture.
7. With a large mixer bowl and clean beaters, beat the egg whites until stiff but not dry. Fold the beaten whites into the ham mixture, adding in thirds. Work quickly and handle gently.
8. Pour the mixture into the soufflé dish. Run thumb around inside edge of dish to make an indentation. This will give the soufflé a top-hat effect. Bake at 375 degrees for 30 minutes. The top will be golden brown. Serve immediately! Serves 4 as a luncheon dish.

Prosciutto and Fontina Sandwich

6 thin slices prosciutto
6 thin slices Fontina
  cheese
6 thin slices onion
6 thick slices tomato
6 thick slices Italian
  bread

6 tablespoons
  mayonnaise
4 tablespoons freshly
  grated Parmesan
  cheese

1. Alternate prosciutto, cheese, onion, and tomato on each slice of bread. Place 1 tablespoon mayonnaise on top of each. Sprinkle with the Parmesan cheese.
2. Lay the sandwiches on a broiler pan. Place 4 inches from broiler element and broil until hot and bubbly. Serves 6.

Hoagie, Philadelphia Style

This is Philadelphia's version of the big Italian sandwich—called Hero, or Poor Boy, or Butcher Boy, or Zep, or Submarine, depending on the city. Nobody knows where the word hoagie came from, though some people insist that this sandwich was originally called a Hoggie, because you felt like a hog after you ate one. That may be true, but it's the kind of answer that only leads to another question. How on earth did the word Hoggie turn into the word Hoagie?

1 hoagie roll (long
  Italian roll), split but
  not cut through
1 tablespoon olive oil
3 slices provolone
  cheese
4 slices salami, hard or
  soft
3 slices capocollo ham

4 tablespoons
  shredded lettuce
3 slices tomato
4–6 thin slices onion
¼ teaspoon oregano
1 tablespoon hot
  peppers, optional

Lay the roll open and drizzle with olive oil. Lay on slices of cheese, salami, capocollo, lettuce, tomatoes, onion, oregano, and hot peppers. Using the back of a large knife, force the filling into roll. Close the roll. Cut in half crosswise. Serves 1.

8

SEAFOOD

EVERY WEDNESDAY WHILE I'M TEACHING AT THE GRITTI
Palace, I get my class up at 6 A.M.—that is, I get as many
as can be convinced or bullied into getting up at 6 A.M.—
and we all go fish shopping with the chefs. The fish market
of Venice is a big marble colonnade with a terrazzo floor
decorated with a splendid mosaic of ferocious-looking fish.
Everything is laid out on tables, shining and fresh from
the sea. Fish stick upright in ice, or are twisted in cork-
screw shapes to trail over the edges of baskets like fat
vines—the better to show they are so fresh they have
rigor mortis and are still firm from the sea.

You will probably never get fish that fresh in America.
And you will probably never get the same variety of fish.
Scampi, which in America is simply shrimp in oil, wine,
butter, and garlic, in Italy is a large prawn or crayfish
indigenous to the Adriatic—usually served broiled, 6–8
to a customer.

But you can substitute American fish easily in most

145

Italian recipes. The recipes are simple—fish is poached, sautéed, or baked and rarely served with a complicated sauce.

Poached Fish Fillets

Serve these fish fillets with lemon wedges and with one of the sauces suggested.

6 fish fillets
  Salt and fresh pepper
  to taste
2 cups water or more

½ cup vinegar
  Butter for greasing
  paper

1. Place the fish fillets in a skillet. Sprinkle with salt and pepper. Add water and vinegar to cover the fish.
2. Lay a piece of buttered parchment or heavy wax paper over the top of the fish. Turn the flame to high, then reduce to medium just before it boils. Simmer 5–10 minutes, depending on the thickness of the fish.
3. Remove the fish and serve with caper sauce (see page 147), pesto (see page 113), tomato sauce I or II (see pages 102–103), sautéed pine nuts, or melted butter and lemon. Serves 6.

Sautéed Fish Fillets

6 fish fillets
½ cup flour
3 tablespoons olive oil

3 tablespoons butter
  Salt and fresh pepper
  to taste.

1. Roll the fish fillets in flour and pat to remove excess.
2. Heat the oil and butter in a large sauté pan and, when the foam subsides, add the fish fillets. Cook 3–4 min-

utes on each side. Season with salt and pepper. Serve with one of the sauces recommended for poached fish. Serves 6.

Fried Basil

Fried parsley is popular, but try frying basil. Excellent and different. Serve with plain broiled fish.

4 cups fresh basil leaves   *Oil for frying*

Pat the basil with a towel so the leaves are not damp. Shred them. Heat the oil to 360–370 degrees. Drop the basil leaves into the hot oil and let cook for 2 minutes. Remove to brown paper to drain.

Caper Sauce

1/3 cup olive oil
Juice of 1/2 lemon
1 garlic clove, chopped
2 tablespoons chopped
  flat-leaf parsley
2 tablespoons chopped
  spinach leaves
1 tablespoon chopped
  scallions
1/4 cup capers, rinsed
Salt and fresh pepper
2 hard-cooked eggs,
  chopped
1/3 cup mayonnaise

Combine everything except the eggs and mayonnaise in a blender jar or food processor. Blend well. Remove the mixture to a bowl. Fold in the eggs and mayonnaise. Serve over poached fish. Makes 1 cup.

Variation

Lighten the sauce by folding in ½ cup heavy cream, whipped.

Baked Fish Fillets

6 fish fillets
  Salt and pepper to
  taste

4 tablespoons butter,
  melted

Lay the fish fillets in a baking dish. Sprinkle with salt and pepper. Drizzle melted butter over the fish. Place in a 425-degree oven and bake for 10 minutes, or until the fish just begins to flake. Serve with one of the sauces recommended for poached fish. Serves 6.

Baked Fish with Olives

1 whole bass or red
  snapper, 3–4 pounds
  cleaned, head and tail
  on
Salt and fresh pepper
  to taste

½ cup olive oil
½ cup vinegar
½ cup white wine
1 cup olives, pits
  removed
Lemon wedges

1. Wash and dry the fish. Sprinkle inside and out with salt and pepper. Lay the fish in a baking dish. Make a slash with a knife down the length of the fish.
2. Sprinkle the fish with olive oil. Add the vinegar and wine. Arrange the olives over and around the fish. Place in a 350-degree oven for about 30 minutes, or until fish begins to flake.
3. Remove the bone, cut the fish into serving pieces, and

serve with the olives and pan juices spooned over.
Serve with lemon wedges. Serves 4–6.

Note: Cook in a 425-degree oven for 15–20 minutes, if
desired.

Fish Baked in Salt

The salt flavor does not penetrate the fish. However, the
fish emerges juicy and extremely flavorful.

*1 fish (2 pounds),
    cleaned, with head
    and tail left on
½ small fennel bulb,
    thinly sliced
Few drops anisette
1 lemon, sliced*

*2 cups coarse salt
2 cups flour
1 cup water,
    approximately
Salt and fresh pepper
    to taste*

1. Place the fennel, anisette, and lemon in the cavity of
   the fish.
2. Combine the salt and flour in a bowl. Add water until
   the mixture holds together.
3. Pat a layer of the salt mixture on the bottom of a
   nonmetal baking dish, ½ inch longer and wider than
   the fish. Smooth the mixture with wet hands. Lay the
   fish on and top with more of the mixture. Smooth with
   wet hands. Bring the top and bottom edges together
   to seal. Pinch tightly all the way around the fish. The
   fish must be completely sealed. With the tip of a knife,
   the edge of a piping tube, or with pastry pincers, make
   decorative scales over the surface of the fish. Place in
   a 375-degree oven and bake for 40 minutes.
4. To serve, cut the pastry lengthwise and push it aside.
   Do not serve or eat the pastry! The fish will be juicy

and succulent. Serve with parsley butter sauce and pepper and salt, if needed. Serves 4–6.

Parsley Butter Sauce

8 tablespoons butter
Juice of 1 lemon

1 tablespoon chopped
flat-leaf parsley

Melt the butter and add lemon juice and parsley. Serve over fish. Makes ½ cup.

Baked Fish Fillets with Blood Oranges

In Italy, blood oranges come from Sicily; in America, from California. In either case, they give this dish a delicious new taste and an attractive bright color. Valencia oranges can also be used.

⅓ cup olive oil
½ cup flour
 6 fish fillets, snapper,
 flounder, or trout
¼ pound mushrooms,
 sliced
 Juice of 1 lemon
½ cup white wine
 Salt and fresh
 pepper to taste

½ cup toasted pine
 nuts (see note)
2–3 blood oranges,
 sectioned
2 tablespoons
 chopped flat-leaf
 parsley

1. Film a baking dish with oil. Flour the fish lightly and arrange in the dish.
2. Scatter the mushrooms over the top of the fish and sprinkle with the lemon juice, white wine, salt, and pepper. Scatter the pine nuts over the surface. Bake 5 minutes in a 350-degree oven.
3. Arrange the orange sections over the top of the fish

and bake another 2–3 minutes. Sprinkle with parsley and serve. Serves 4–6.

Note: To toast pine nuts, lay them on a baking sheet. Bake at 350 degrees for 10 minutes.

Swordfish with Caper Butter

8 tablespoons butter
Juice of 1 lemon
4 tablespoons capers,
  washed and drained
2 tablespoons finely
  chopped flat-leaf
  parsley

6 swordfish steaks, 1
  inch thick
Lemon wedges

1. Melt the butter in a small pan. Add the lemon juice, capers, and parsley.
2. Lay the swordfish steaks on a baking dish. Brush the steaks with half the butter mixture. Bake at 400 degrees for 10 minutes, basting once. The fish should barely flake. Cook another minute or so if better done is preferred.
3. Pour the rest of the butter mixture over the fish and serve with lemon wedges. Serves 6.

Variations

Substitute salmon, flounder, trout, or halibut for the swordfish.

Serve anchovy butter made by sautéeing 6 anchovies in 8 tablespoons butter.

Stuffed Small Fish

3 cups fresh bread
crumbs
¼ cup milk
2 tablespoons butter
1 onion, chopped
¼ cup chopped flat-leaf
parsley
2 garlic cloves, chopped
2 eggs
¼ cup grated Pecorino
or Parmesan cheese
2 tablespoons pine nuts
or chopped walnuts
(optional)

2 tablespoons raisins
(optional)
Salt and fresh pepper
to taste
Olive oil
16 fresh sardines, red
mullet, butterfish,
smelts, spots, or
sunfish, boned and
split open
Lemon wedges

1. Place the bread crumbs in a bowl. Add the milk and let soak.
2. Melt the butter and sauté the onion until limp. Add the parsley and garlic and cook 1 minute longer
3. Squeeze the bread to release the milk and add bread to the onion mixture. Mix thoroughly. Add the eggs, cheese, nuts, and raisins. The mixture should be pasty. Season with salt and pepper.
4. Film a baking dish with olive oil. Lay the fish on a flat surface, opened up, skin side down, and spoon some stuffing on each. Re-form the fish and lay close together in the baking dish. Drizzle a little olive oil over the top.
5. Bake in a 350-degree oven for 15–20 minutes until done. Baste once while cooking. Serve with lemon wedges. Serves 4–6.

Variations

Sandwich two fish together. Open the fish. Stuff one and do not re-form. Place another opened fish on top.

A bit of tomato sauce can be spooned over the fish before baking.

Mix together dried bread crumbs, parsley, and grated Pecorino cheese. Sprinkle over the fish with a little olive oil before baking.

If small fish are unavailable, sandwich the stuffing between two fillets of fish.

Sweet and Sour Flounder

This is a very popular Venetian recipe. I do not usually like nuts and raisins in my food, but here it is classic.

6 small flounder fillets,
  cut lengthwise in two.
½ cup flour
½ cup olive oil
3 large onions, thinly
  sliced
1 tablespoon sugar
½ cup white wine
  vinegar

Salt and fresh pepper
  to taste
¼ cup raisins
¼ cup pine nuts
2 tablespoons chopped
  flat-leaf parsley

1. Roll the flounder in the flour. Pat off excess.
2. Heat the olive oil in a sauté pan. Cook the fillets 1 minute on one side. Carefully turn them over and cook the other side for 2–3 minutes, or until the fish just flakes. Remove the fish to a platter.
3. Add the onions to the pan and stir around with a wooden spatula. Add the sugar and cook 10 minutes on a medium fire, stirring until the onions are soft. Add the vinegar, salt, pepper, raisins, and pine nuts and cook a few minutes to soften the raisins.
4. Pour the onion mixture over the fish. Sprinkle with the parsley. Serve hot or at room temperature. Serves 6.

Codfish and Vermouth

6 cod fillets, or use
halibut, whiting, or
monkfish
2 tablespoons olive oil
Salt and fresh pepper
to taste
Few sprigs oregano

2 tablespoons chopped
flat-leaf parsley
2 tablespoons blanched
slivered almonds or
pine nuts
½ cup dry vermouth
Lemon wedges

1. Brush the cod fillets with oil. Lay in a baking dish. Sprinkle with salt, pepper, oregano, and parsley. Scatter nuts on top. Pour vermouth around the fish.
2. Bake at 350 degrees for 10 minutes, or until fish just begins to flake. Serve the fish from the dish and spoon the juices over. Serve with lemon wedges. Serves 6.

Fried Mussels

4 dozen mussels,
cleaned, bearded,
steamed in wine,
opened, and removed
from the shells
1 cup dry bread crumbs
½ cup freshly grated
Parmesan or Pecorino
cheese

Finely chopped flat-
leaf parsley
1 cup flour
2 eggs, beaten
Oil for frying
Lemon wedges

1. Dry the mussels on a towel.
2. Mix together the bread crumbs, cheese, and parsley.
3. Roll the mussels, a few at a time, in flour, next in the beaten egg, then in the bread crumbs.
4. Heat the oil to 360–370 degrees and fry the mussels, a few at a time, until crisp and brown, 2–3 minutes. Drain on brown paper. Serve with lemon wedges. Serves 4–6.

Variation

This recipe is equally good with oysters or clams.

Sautéed Sardines

12–16 fresh sardines,	*8 tablespoons butter*
cleaned, split,	*Salt and fresh pepper*
and boned	*to taste*
1 cup milk	*Lemon wedges*
1 cup bread crumbs	

1. Dip the sardines in milk, then in bread crumbs.
2. Melt the butter in a skillet. When the foam subsides, sauté the fish, a few at a time, 2–3 minutes on each side. Season with salt and pepper. Serve with lemon wedges. Serves 4–6.

Note: Small spots, butterfish, or smelts may be prepared this way.

Variations

12–16 fresh sardines,	*Salt and fresh pepper to*
cleaned and	*taste*
heads removed	*Lemon wedges*
½ cup olive oil	

Broiled fresh sardines. Coat the sardines with the oil seasoned with salt and pepper. Lay on a broiler rack. Broil 2 minutes on each side, 4 inches from the heat element. Serve with lemon wedges. Serves 4–6.

Fried sardines. Dip sardines in ½ cup flour, then in beaten egg and bread crumbs. Fry in hot fat (360 degrees) for 3–5 minutes, or until brown and cooked through. Serve plain or with a tomato sauce.

Baked Oysters with Pesto

1 pound rock salt,
   approximately
24 oysters on the half
   shell
1 recipe pesto (see page
   113)

½ cup dry bread crumbs
4 tablespoons butter,
   melted

1. Arrange rock salt on a foil-lined baking sheet. Place in a 400-degree oven for 10–15 minutes to heat the salt.
2. Lay the oysters on the hot salt and spoon some pesto onto each. Sprinkle each oyster with bread crumbs and drizzle a little melted butter over each.
3. Broil 5 minutes, 3 inches from the heating unit, or bake at 400 degrees for 5–7 minutes. Do not overcook or the oysters will be rubbery. Serves 4–6.

Variation

Substitute clams for oysters.

Shrimp with Fennel

2 pounds baby shrimp,
   cooked in the shell
2 celery ribs, finely
   chopped
1 small fennel bulb,
   trimmed and julienned
Salt and fresh pepper
to taste

4 tablespoons chopped
   flat-leaf parsley
Juice of 2 large
   lemons
½ cup olive oil
2 heads Bibb lettuce, or
   1 head Boston lettuce,
   washed and dried

1. Place the shrimp, celery, fennel, salt, pepper, and parsley in a large bowl. Squeeze the lemon juice over and

mix well. Add the oil and mix again. Place in the refrigerator for 10 minutes or so.
2. Arrange the lettuce on a large platter. Fill the lettuce cups with the shrimp mixture. Serves 4–6.

Note: To make the platter more attractive, arrange black olives around the edge. This is also good with slivers of mozzarella cheese added.

Shrimp Portofino Style

A very unusual combination, but very good when the grapefruit are at their best. I adapted this recipe from La Manuelina restaurant in Ricco, just outside Genoa.

½ cup olive oil	Salt and fresh pepper
2 pounds medium	to taste
shrimp, cleaned	2 teaspoons sugar
Juice of 2 grapefruits	1 teaspoon flour
Juice of 2 lemons	¼ cup Cognac

1. Heat the olive oil in a sauté pan. Add the shrimp and sauté 2 minutes.
2. Add the grapefruit and lemon juice, salt, and pepper. Cook on a high flame for 3 more minutes, or until the shrimp are pink. Stir to keep the shrimp from sticking.
3. Reduce the flame. Add the sugar and sprinkle on the flour. Stir 1 minute. Set the sauté pan off the heat. Heat the Cognac and ignite. Pour over the shrimp. When the flame burns out, serve the shrimp. Serves 4–6.

Scampi

12–16 large shrimp
1 cup olive oil
¼ cup dry white
 wine
2 tablespoons
 chopped flat-leaf
 parsley

4 garlic cloves, chopped
Salt and fresh pepper
 to taste
Lemon wedges

1. Split the shrimp shells up the back with a small sharp knife. Devein and shell, if desired.
2. Heat the oil in a large skillet. When hot, add the shrimp and cook, while stirring, 3 minutes.
3. Sprinkle the wine, parsley, garlic, salt, and pepper over the shrimp. Cook 3 minutes longer. Serve at once with lemon wedges. Serves 3–4.

Broiled Scampi

20 very large shrimp in
 the shell
Olive oil or melted
 butter
Salt and fresh pepper
 to taste

Juice of 2 lemons
2 tablespoons chopped
 flat-leaf parsley

1. Split the shrimp down the back and open out flat. Remove the vein. Lay open side up on a baking sheet.
2. Brush with oil or melted butter, salt, and pepper. Squeeze lemon juice over. Broil 4 inches from heating unit about 3 minutes. Sprinkle with parsley and serve in the shells. Serves 4–6.

Shrimp with Green Sauce

2 pounds medium shrimp
  in shells
2 tablespoons vinegar
1 tablespoon salt
  Few hot pepper flakes

2 dozen very small new
  potatoes, boiled
  Green sauce (see
  following recipe)

1. Place the shrimp in a pan and cover with water. Add
   the vinegar, salt, and hot pepper flakes. Bring to a boil.
   Immediately turn to a simmer and cook 2–3 minutes,
   until shrimp turn pink. Remove the shrimp.
2. Peel when the shrimp are cool enough to handle.
   Arrange the shrimp in one serving dish, potatoes in
   another, and put the green sauce in a serving bowl.
   Serves 4–6.

Green Sauce

This is the popular salsa verde served with boiled meat
or fish.

4 anchovies, washed,
  dried, and chopped
1 hard-cooked egg yolk
2 tablespoons bread
  crumbs
½ cup white wine
  vinegar
1 large garlic clove,
  chopped

½ cup chopped flat-leaf
  parsley
1 tablespoon capers
1 cup olive oil
  Salt and pepper to
  taste

1. Put the anchovies, egg yolk, bread crumbs and vinegar
   in a small bowl. Mash with a spoon.

2. Add the garlic, parsley, and capers and begin adding the oil slowly while mixing with a wooden spoon. Keep stirring until all the oil is mixed in. Taste and season with salt and pepper, if necessary. A little hot pepper is sometimes added. Makes a good 1½ cups.

Marinated Squid

2–3 pounds squid, cleaned, quill and skin removed, and cut into rings
⅔ cup olive oil
Juice of 2 lemons
2 tablespoons chopped flat-leaf parsley

2–3 leaves fresh basil, chopped
Salt and fresh pepper to taste

1. Drop the squid rings into boiling water. Cook on medium heat until tender, 15–20 minutes. Drain.
2. Place the squid in a bowl. Pour the oil, lemon juice, parsley, and basil over them. Season with salt and pepper. Toss and serve tepid. Serves 4–6.

Stuffed Squid

Squid is available everywhere, even in the frozen food case of most supermarkets. It is plentiful, cheap, and has a distinct and delicate flavor. Many people still shy away from it, possibly because they had those tough little breaded rubber bands served as squid in some restaurants. If squid is properly cooked, it is not tough. Try it and see.

6 tablespoons olive oil	2–3 leaves fresh basil, chopped
1 large onion, chopped	Salt and fresh pepper to taste
2 green peppers, seeded and cut into chunks	2–3 pounds squid, cleaned, quill removed, and, tentacles chopped and reserved
2 red peppers, seeded and cut into chunks	
1 garlic clove, chopped	½ cup white or red wine
2 tablespoons chopped flat-leaf parsley	3 bay leaves

1. Heat 4 tablespoons of the olive oil. Add the onion, green and red pepper, garlic, and parsley. Cook 3–4 minutes.
2. Put in a food processor and blend but leave a bit chunky.
3. Transfer the mixture to a bowl and add the basil, salt, pepper, and reserved tentacles. Stuff some of the mixture into the squid. Close the tops with toothpicks.
4. Place the stuffed squid in a baking dish. Sprinkle with the remaining 2 tablespoons oil, the wine, bay leaves, and any remaining stuffing. Place in a 375-degree oven and bake 30 minutes. Discard the toothpicks and bay leaves. Serve the squid with the juices. Serves 4–6.

Note: After the squid are cleaned, lay them a few at a time on a griddle over high heat for 1 minute, or until they expand.

Fried Squid

Oil for frying
2–3 pounds, squid,
    cleaned, quill and
    skin removed, sliced
    into circles, and
    tentacles reserved

1 cup flour
2 eggs, beaten
1 cup bread crumbs
Lemon wedges for
    garnish

1. Heat the oil to 360–370 degrees
2. Dry the squid thoroughly.
3. Roll the squid rings in flour, dip in the beaten egg, and roll in bread crumbs. Drop a few at a time into the hot oil and cook 3–5 minutes, until brown and crisp.
4. Coat the tentacles with flour, egg, and crumbs and fry them 1–2 minutes. Drain. Serve with lemon wedges. Serves 4–6.

Tuna Sauce

1 can (medium size)
    Italian tuna fish
12 anchovies, washed
    and drained
2 cups homemade
    mayonnaise (see page
    27)

White wine
Cooked veal slices,
    chicken breast, turkey
    breast, or fish fillets
Capers
Lemon slices

1. Purée the tuna fish and 2 anchovies in a food processor. Add to the homemade mayonnaise. Thin to napping consistency with white wine.
2. Spoon a thin layer of tuna mayonnaise in a serving dish. Layer thin slices of veal, chicken, turkey, or fish fillets over it. Spoon over more of the tuna mayonnaise. Crisscross remaining anchovies on the top, sprinkle with a few capers, and edge the dish with thin slices of lemon. Chill before serving. Serves 4–6.

9

MEAT AND POULTRY

UP AROUND FLORENCE, WHERE CATTLE ARE RAISED for beef, they cut big slabs of meat—something like our T-bone steaks—brush them with oil, run them under the broiler, and serve with a wedge of lemon. Sometimes you get a bit of butter to add at the table. Throughout the rest of Italy, beef is cut into small pieces to use for involtini, or braciole. Beef is not very cheap, and not very common, in Italy.

But veal is, and Italian chefs always pound veal, no matter how tender the cut. And when they pound, they pound hard, but carefully. A chop is sometimes butterflied right along the bone, put between two sheets of wax paper, and then just slammed and slammed until it spreads out symmetrically around the bone into one big tender piece of meat, almost large enough to cover the plate. If you want to pound veal like a true Italian chef, put it between two sheets of wax paper and pound at it until you feel one more smack at the meat and you'll go through the table. But no holes, please. Some chefs prefer to use a wooden mallet, which they wet and slide as they pound; others simply use the bottom of a pan, cast iron or aluminum, the heavier the better.

Baby lamb in spring really is baby lamb in Italy. I still remember the first time I ordered a leg of lamb from the kitchen to demonstrate a roast that would serve six at a formal supper. In came a tiny little thing no bigger than a turkey drumstick. I had to order six more and braise them with lots of vegetables so everybody in the class could at least get a taste. Lamb as young as Italian lamb is always served well done—otherwise it wouldn't have any flavor.

The chickens of Italy taste wonderful simply roasted with a sprig of rosemary in the cavity—the chickens get to run around the farmyard so they develop more flavor, and the rosemary is gathered wild, full of perfume from Italian hills. I order this dish again and again when I'm in Venice, and I make it sometimes when I come back home and find fresh-killed chicken in a farmer's market and fresh rosemary in my vegetable store. It reminds me of Italy. But it's never the same.

Italians fry chicken by chopping it into small bite-size pieces, giving it an extra thick coating of batter, and serving with lemon. You don't have to cut your chicken into such small bits to make Italian fried chicken—but if you take the trouble, you'll find it tastes better somehow. Maybe because it's so much more crunchy.

Turkey breast is very popular in Italy. Italians love the stuff, and treat it just like chicken or veal; pound it, roll it, stuff it, layer it with truffles and Fontina cheese, and, of course, serve it the way almost all protein is served in Italy, with lots of fresh lemon wedges.

Whole turkey is popular, too. Each year, besides cooking classes in Italian cooking for Americans, I teach one class in American cooking for Italians. And the first thing all the Italians want to know is how to make a Thanksgiving turkey, with all the trimmings: stuffing, giblet gravy, mashed potatoes, candied sweet potatoes, cranberry sauce, creamed onions. To them, it's the most exotic food in the world. The second thing they all want to know how to make is—lemon meringue pie. I have a terrible suspicion that some of my students serve the pie right along with the turkey when they make their Thanksgiving feast, because they have to have some kind of lemon with meat; but I'm never around to find out.

Stuffed Veal Chops

Chops can be stuffed with anything as long as you add either beaten egg or cheese to bind the mixture.

¼ cup diced prosciutto or other ham
¼ pound mushrooms, sliced
¼ cup diced Fontina cheese
Salt and fresh pepper to taste
5–6 basil leaves, chopped

6 loin veal chops, 1 inch thick
4 tablespoons butter
4 tablespoons chopped scallions
¼ cup heavy cream
2 tablespoons red wine

1. Mix in a bowl the ham, mushrooms, cheese, salt, pepper, and half the basil.
2. Make a slit in each chop for a pocket. Stuff the mixture into the chops. Pinch the open edges together.
3. Melt the butter in a skillet. When hot, brown the chops about 3 minutes on each side. Season with salt and pepper. Remove the chops and keep warm.
4. Add the scallions to the pan and cook a minute or two. Add the heavy cream, remaining basil, and wine. Stir and put the chops back in the pan. Cook, covered, 10–15 minutes on medium heat.
5. Remove the cover. Turn the chops and cook 10 minutes longer, or until the chops are tender. Reduce the sauce to thicken, if necessary. Serves 6.

Breaded Veal Chops

6 rib veal chops, ¾ inch thick	2 tablespoons oil
1 cup flour	4 tablespoons butter
3 eggs, beaten	Salt and fresh pepper to taste
1 cup bread crumbs	Lemon wedges

1. Place the veal chops on foil. Dip a mallet in ice water. Pound the chops gently until they are reduced to ¼ inch thick.
2. Place the flour, beaten eggs, and bread crumbs in separate dishes or plates. Dip each chop in the flour and pat off excess. Dip in the beaten egg and finally dip in the crumbs.
3. Heat the oil and the butter in a large skillet. When hot, sauté the chops on moderate heat for 3–5 minutes on each side. Season with salt and pepper. Serve hot with lemon wedges. Serves 6.

Veal Parmesan, American Style

I have never seen this dish in Italy. I suspect that it originated from eggplant Parmesan when meat was more plentiful in America than in southern Italy.

8–12 veal scallops (3 by 5 inches), cut very thin	1½ cups tomato sauce I or II (see pages 102–103)
2 eggs, slightly beaten	Salt and fresh pepper to taste
¾ cup dry bread crumbs	½ pound mozzarella, sliced
3–4 tablespoons butter	Freshly grated Parmesan cheese

1. Dip the veal in the beaten egg and then in the bread crumbs.
2. Heat the butter in a skillet and, when foam subsides, add the veal. Brown on each side, about 6 minutes altogether.
3. In the bottom of a 1½-quart shallow baking dish, place half the tomato sauce. Arrange the veal on the sauce in one layer. Season with salt and pepper. Arrange the mozzarella over the veal. Pour the rest of the tomato sauce over the veal. Sprinkle with Parmesan cheese.
4. Bake at 350 degrees until the cheese melts and the veal is heated through. Serves 4–6.

Breaded Veal Cutlet

1 egg	2 tablespoons oil
2 tablespoons milk	2 tablespoons butter
1½ pounds veal cutlet, pounded	Salt and fresh pepper to taste
Flour	1 tablespoon chopped parsley
¾ cup dry bread crumbs	Lemon wedges

1. Beat the egg and milk together.
2. Remove any extra fat or tough skin around the edge of the cutlets. Lightly dust the cutlets with flour. Dip first in the egg and milk mixture and then in the bread crumbs.
3. Heat the oil and butter in a large sauté pan. Sauté each cutlet on medium-high heat until a dark golden brown on both sides. Lift with a wide spatula and remove from the pan. Season with salt and pepper and garnish with parsley and lemon wedges. Serves 4–6.

Veal Steak with Lemon

2 tablespoons butter
1 veal steak, bone in,
    about 2 pounds, 1 inch
    thick
1 garlic clove, chopped
    Salt and fresh pepper
    to taste

3–4 basil leaves,
    chopped
    Juice of 1 lemon
1 teaspoon grated
    lemon peel
¾ cup chicken stock

1. Melt the butter in a skillet. When the foam subsides, add the veal and brown quickly on each side.
2. Add the remaining ingredients, cover pan, and cook at a low simmer for 12–15 minutes. Remove veal and keep warm.
3. Raise the heat and reduce the liquid in the pan until syrupy. Spoon over steak. Serves 4–6.

Veal Chops with Basil

2 tablespoons oil
6 loin veal chops, 1 inch
    thick
    Salt and fresh pepper
    to taste
1 garlic clove, chopped

¼ cup chopped basil
    leaves
¾ cup white wine
    Juice of 1 lemon
4 tablespoons butter

1. Heat the oil in a large skillet. Brown the chops for 3 minutes one each side, or until golden. Season the chops with salt and pepper and remove from the pan.
2. Add the garlic, basil, and wine to the pan. Add the chops and cook, covered, for 20 minutes. Transfer the chops to a platter.

3. Add lemon juice to the pan. Reduce the sauce by half. Swirl in the butter, bit by bit, and pour the sauce over the chops. Serves 6.

Rolled Veal Scallops

3 cups fresh bread crumbs
2 tablespoons chopped flat-leaf parsley
¼ cup freshly grated Parmesan cheese
5 tablespoons butter
1 cup chopped celery
½ cup chopped onion
Salt and fresh pepper to taste

1½ pounds veal scallops, 4 by 6 inches, ⅛ inch thick
4–5 tablespoons oil
¼ cup vermouth
1½ cups tomato sauce I or II (see pages 102–103)
¼ cup pesto sauce (see page 113)

1. Place the bread crumbs, parsley, and cheese in a bowl.
2. Melt the butter in a large fry pan. Add the chopped celery, onion, salt, and pepper. Cook until the vegetables are crunchy and glossy. Add to the bread crumb and parsley mixture. Mix thoroughly. Taste for seasoning.
3. Place each veal scallop on a board. With a cleaver or pounder slightly moistened, pound each scallop to a larger size. Place 2 tablespoons bread stuffing down the center. Starting at the pointed end, roll each scallop and tie. Place the veal on a tray ready to be browned.
4. Heat a large sauté pan on high and, when hot, add 2 tablespoons of oil. Lower the heat to medium high. Add the veal rolls, a few at a time so they are not touching. Carefully turn them over as they brown on all sides. Remove to a shallow baking dish. Finish browning the remaining veal rolls, adding oil as needed.

5. After all are cooked, remove the strings. Add vermouth to the pan and cook for 1 minute. Strain the juice over the top of a veal.
6. Spoon tomato sauce mixed with ¼ cup of pesto sauce over the veal. Bake, covered, in a 350-degree oven for 10–15 minutes, or until tender. Serves 4–6.

Veal Scaloppine

1½ pounds veal
   scallops, 4 by 6
   inches and ⅛ inch
   thick
Salt and fresh
   pepper to taste
Flour for dusting
   veal

2 tablespoons butter
2 tablespoons oil
¼ cup chicken stock
¼ cup dry Marsala
2 tablespoons chopped
   flat-leaf parsley

1. Use a cleaver or pounder moistened with water and pound the veal scallops until thin and larger in size. Sprinkle with salt and pepper and dust with flour. Place on a platter until ready to sauté.
2. Heat a large skillet until hot, add part of the butter and oil, and sauté scallops, a few at a time, not touching, until lightly brown, 2 to 3 minutes on each side. Remove and keep warm in the oven while finishing the remaining pieces of veal in the remaining butter and oil.
3. After all the pieces are cooked, add the chicken stock and Marsala, stirring with a wooden spoon to scrape up any brown bits. Boil 1–2 minutes to reduce.
4. Put the sautéed veal into the sauce. Simmer for 5 minutes and serve sprinkled with chopped parsley. Serves 4–6.

Veal Roll

Any leftovers are good cold the following day.

1½ pounds veal
  cutlet, flattened
  Salt and fresh
  pepper to taste
1 teaspoon grated
  lemon rind
3 or 4 slices prosciutto
½ pound mozzarella
  cheese, thinly
  sliced

2 hard-cooked eggs,
  peeled
2 tablespoons
  chopped flat-leaf
  parsley
1–2 sage leaves,
  chopped
2 tablespoons butter
1 cup dry white wine

1. Lay the flattened veal on a board. Season with salt, pepper, and lemon rind. Cover with prosciutto and then the sliced cheese. Lay the eggs on top side by side. Sprinkle with parsley and sage. Roll lengthwise and tie in several places.
2. Melt the butter in a baking pan or casserole. When the foam subsides, add the meat and brown on all sides.
3. Add the wine, bring to a boil, and cover the casserole. Bake in a 350-degree oven until the meat is less tender, 45 minutes.
4. To serve, remove the strings and cut the veal into slices. Reduce the juices in the casserole and pour over the veal slices. Serves 4–6.

Veal Patties with Capers

A great change from hamburgers.

1½ pounds ground veal
3 tablespoons chopped parsley
3 tablespoons chopped scallions
Bread crumbs from 2 slices fresh bread without crusts
3 tablespoons milk
⅓ cup drained and rinsed capers, chopped fine

Salt and fresh pepper to taste
3 tablespoons dry bread crumbs
3 tablespoons vegetable oil
1 cup light cream
2 tablespoons chopped parsley for garnish

1. Mix the ground veal with the 3 tablespoons parsley, scallions, fresh bread crumbs that have been soaked in milk, chopped capers, salt, and fresh ground pepper. Mix well and shape into 12 medium-size patties. Roll in dry bread crumbs.
2. Sauté the patties in three batches, using 1 tablespoon oil for each batch. Brown the patties on each side, remove, and keep warm in a 200-degree oven until all are cooked.
3. After all the patties are finished, add the cream to the pan, scraping up bits and mixing well. Pour over the veal patties and sprinkle with chopped parsley. Serves 4–6.

Roast Loin of Veal

This is an expensive cut of veal, but elegant for company and easy to slice.

1 loin of veal, 2½ to 3
  pounds
  Salt and fresh pepper
  to taste

1 garlic clove, mashed
  Olive oil
½ cup white wine
½ cup melted butter

1. Tie the meat every 2 inches so it will hold its shape. Rub the meat with salt, pepper, and garlic clove.
2. Heat the oil in a skillet and brown the meat on all sides.
3. Place on a rack in a roasting pan. Roast at 375 degrees for 40–45 minutes, or until a meat thermometer registers 160 degrees. Baste twice with wine and butter.
4. Let rest 10 minutes to settle the juices. Remove the strings. Carve into thin slices. Serve with the pan juices. Serves 4–6.

Variation

Veal with basil cream. Pour off all the pan juices. Deglaze the pan with ½ cup vermouth. Add 1½ cups heavy cream and ½ cup shredded basil. Cook to reduce the cream by half. Spoon over the veal slices.

Veal with Mushrooms

4 tablespoons butter
1½ pounds veal
  scallops, pounded
¼ cup finely chopped
  onion
1 cup mushrooms,
  cleaned and sliced

½ cup dry vermouth
½ cup chicken stock
1 cup heavy cream
  Salt and fresh pepper
  to taste

1. Heat the butter in a large skillet. When the foam subsides, sauté the veal quickly (2 minutes) on both sides. Remove the veal from the pan.

2. Add the onion and mushrooms to the fat in the pan. Cook, while stirring with a wooden spatula, 3 minutes.
3. Add the vermouth and chicken stock. Reduce to half.
4. Add the heavy cream and bring to a boil. Reduce the heat, add the veal, and cook on moderate heat 10 minutes. Season with salt and pepper. Serves 4–6.

Veal Marsala

Always use dry Marsala wine in veal Marsala. Some Italian restaurants in the United States use sweet Marsala, which gives this dish a syrupy flavor it just doesn't need.

6–8 thin slices of veal, pounded
3 tablespoons butter
½ cup chicken stock
¼ cup dry Marsala
Salt and fresh pepper to taste
Juice of ½ lemon

1. Sauté the veal in the butter 2–3 minutes on each side. Remove the veal.
2. Add the chicken stock, Marsala, salt, and pepper and bring to a boil. Reduce.
3. Add the lemon juice and pour over the veal. Serves 4–6.

Minute Steaks with Olives

3 tablespoons oil
6 minute steaks, ¾-inch thick
Salt and fresh pepper to taste
1 garlic clove, chopped
1 cup tomatoes, peeled, seeded, and chopped
2 tablespoons chopped scallions
¼ cup pitted and chopped black olives
1 tablespoon capers, drained
2 tablespoons dry Marsala

1. Heat the oil in a heavy skillet. Sauté the steaks 1–2 minutes on each side. Sprinkle with salt and pepper.
2. Remove the steaks from the pan and add the remaining ingredients. Bring to a boil. Put the steaks in the sauce and cook 5 minutes, or until tender. Serves 6.

Braciole

This dish is usually made as a big meat roll in America and sliced into portions. In Italy it is usually made in individual servings, and the result is easier to handle, tastes even better, and makes more sense for today's smaller families. I learned this version from a chef from Bari, the provincial capital of Puglia, so this dish is an example of real down-home Southern cooking, Italian style.

8 pieces beef round, 5 by 3 by ¼ inches
3 garlic cloves, chopped
¼ pound prosciutto, cut into 8 pieces
¼ pound Pecorino cheese, cut into 8 pieces
¼ cup chopped flat-leaf parsley

Salt and fresh pepper to taste
4 tablespoons olive oil
1 large onion, chopped
¾ cup red wine
3 ripe tomatoes, peeled, seeded, and chopped

1. Flatten the beef as for veal scallops by placing each slice between pieces of wax paper and pounding with a cleaver or a skillet.
2. On each piece of beef, place some of the garlic, a piece of prosciutto, a piece of Pecorino cheese, and parsley. Season with salt and pepper. Roll up and tie with string.
3. Heat the oil in a casserole. Sauté the beef until brown. Remove.
4. Add the onion and sauté for 3 minutes.

5. Add the wine and tomatoes. Cook on top of the stove for 3 minutes more.
6. Put the beef back in the casserole. Bake, covered, at 350 degrees for 45 minutes, or until the beef is tender. Remove the strings. Remove fat from sauce, pour over beef, and serve. Serves 4–6.

Steak with Marsala

6 shell, Delmonico, or
sirloin strip steaks cut
¼ inch thick
Salt and fresh pepper
to taste
6 tablespoons butter

2 tablespoons Cognac
4 tablespoons dry
Marsala
2 tablespoons chopped
flat-leaf parsley

1. Pound the steaks with a wet mallet, or between two sheets of wax paper, as thin as possible without tearing the meat. Sprinkle with salt and pepper.
2. Melt 4 tablespoons of the butter in a sauté pan. When the foam subsides, sear the steaks 1 minute on each side. Place on a serving platter.
3. Pour off the fat from the pan. Add the Cognac and flame. Add the Marsala and swirl the pan on heat for 1 minute. Add the remaining 2 tablespoons butter and swirl the pan until the butter melts. Pour over the meat. Garnish with parsley. Serves 6.

Variation

After sautéeing the steaks for 1 minute on each side, serve with Carlo's pizzaiola sauce poured over (see following recipe).

Carlo's Pizzaiola Sauce

¼ cup olive oil
2–3 garlic cloves,
   chopped
4 cups tomatoes,
   peeled, seeded, and
   chopped
4 tablespoons
   chopped flat-leaf
   parsley

Salt and fresh pepper
   to taste
1 teaspoon oregano
½ cup dry white wine
   (optional)

1. Heat the oil in a large saucepan. When hot, add the garlic and stir until it is limp, about 2 minutes.
2. Add the remaining ingredients and cook 20 minutes, uncovered, stirring frequently. Serve over pasta, meat, and fish. Serves 4–6.

Note: Meat or fish can be cooked in the sauce, if desired.

Meatballs and Mushrooms

4 slices white bread,
   crusts removed
1 cup milk
1 medium-size onion,
   chopped
6 tablespoons butter
1 pound ground round
   beef
½ pound ground veal
½ pound ground lean
   pork

2 eggs
2 tablespoons chopped
   mixed parsley and
   basil
Salt and fresh
   pepper to taste
1 pound mushrooms
1½ cups heavy cream
½ cup red wine

1. Crumble the bread into a large mixing bowl. Soak it in milk.

2. Sauté the onion in 2 tablespoons of the butter until soft but not brown. Add it to the bread.
3. Add the meat, eggs, chopped herbs, salt, and pepper. Blend thoroughly but lightly. Form into balls.
4. Heat the remaining 4 tablespoons of butter in the same skillet. Cook the meatballs, a single layer at a time, until browned all over. As they are browned, place them in a baking dish.
5. Slice the mushroom caps and lightly brown them in the skillet. Add the cream and stir until it comes to a boil. Add the red wine and season with salt and pepper. Pour over the meat.
6. Cook, uncovered, in a 350-degree oven until well heated, about 30 minutes. Serves 6–8.

Meatballs with Pine Nuts

1½ pounds ground meat, a combination of beef, veal, and pork
2 eggs
2 slices bread, crumbled
½ cup milk
2 tablespoons grated onion
⅓ cup chopped flat-leaf parsley
½ cup toasted pine nuts
½ cup dry bread crumbs
Salt and fresh pepper to taste
6–8 tablespoons vegetable oil
¾ cup dry vermouth

1. Mix the combined meats with the eggs, bread that has been soaked in milk, grated onion, chopped parsley, pine nuts, dry bread crumbs, salt, and pepper.
2. To prepare the meatballs for frying, use a small ice cream dipper (size 40). This is equivalent to 2 tablespoons. Otherwise, a full rounded tablespoon of meat

mixture is equivalent to 2 tablespoons. Place the meatballs on a tray ready to fry. Place in the refrigerator
for 15 minutes, if you have time.

3. Cook the meatballs in four batches, using 2 tablespoons of oil and about 7 meatballs in each batch.
Shake the pan back and forth and, with a wooden
spatula, turn them around so they brown on all sides.
Remove the meatballs to an ovenware dish. Keep warm
in a 200-degree oven while continuing to cook the
remaining meatballs.

4. Add the vermouth to the pan, scraping up the loose
pine nuts and brown bits. Reduce to half. Stir quickly
and pour over the cooked meatballs. Serves 4–6.

Meat-Stuffed Zucchini

Good as an appetizer.

8 small zucchini
1 pound ground beef,
    pork, or veal, or any
    combination
1 egg
2 garlic cloves, chopped
    Salt and fresh pepper
    to taste
½ teaspoon chopped
    fresh oregano
2 slices bread, crusts
    removed, crumbled
¼ cup olive oil
2 tablespoons chopped
    flat-leaf parsley

1. Wash and dry the zucchini. Trim off the ends. Remove
the centers with an apple corer or a thin-bladed knife.
Chop the centers and set aside.

2. Mix the ground meat in a bowl with the egg, garlic,
salt, pepper, oregano, chopped zucchini, and the bread,
which has been soaked in water and squeezed dry.

3. Combine these ingredients well and put into a pastry
bag fitted with a plain tube. Pipe the mixture into the
zucchini shells from both ends.

4. Sauté the zucchini in olive oil for 3 minutes, until lightly browned.
5. Arrange them in a small baking dish and pour the oil from the pan over them. Bake for 20 minutes at 350 degrees until tender. To serve, sprinkle with the chopped parsley. Serve hot or at room temperature. Serves 4–6.

Pork Chops Alla Santina

6 tablespoons oil
6 loin pork chops, 1 inch thick
2 red peppers, seeded and cut into thin strips
2 garlic cloves, chopped
2 ripe tomatoes, peeled, seeded, and chopped
Salt and fresh pepper to taste
½ pound mushrooms, sliced

1. Heat the oil in a large skillet. Add the chops and brown quickly, 1–2 minutes on each side. Remove from the pan and keep warm.
2. Add the peppers, garlic, and tomatoes to the oil remaining in the pan. Season with salt and pepper. Cook, while stirring, for 5 minutes.
3. Return the chops to the pan, cover, reduce heat, and cook for 15 minutes.
4. Turn the chops, add the mushrooms, and cook 10 more minutes. Serve the chops with the vegetables on top. Serves 6.

Variation

Substitute chicken pieces for pork chops.

Pork Chops with Peppers

4 peppers, green and
red, seeds and
filaments removed
4 tablespoons olive oil
1 garlic clove, chopped
1 onion, chopped
6 loin pork chops, ¾
inch thick
1 cup peeled, seeded,
and chopped
tomatoes

2 or 3 sage leaves,
chopped
¾ cup white or red wine
Salt and fresh pepper
to taste
4 tablespoons freshly
grated Parmesan
cheese

1. Cut the peppers into strips.
2. Heat the oil in a large skillet. Add the peppers, garlic, and onion. Stir with a wooden spatula for 5 minutes. Remove the vegetables and set aside.
3. In the oil remaining in the pan, sauté the pork chops 2–3 minutes on each side. Remove to a casserole or baking dish.
4. Add the tomatoes, sage, wine, salt, and pepper to the pan. Bring to a boil, scraping the pan. Boil 2 minutes. Pour over the chops. Add the peppers and onion. Mix well.
5. Place in a 350-degree oven and bake 30–40 minutes, until chops are very tender. Sprinkle the cheese over the chops during the last 15 minutes of baking. Serves 6.

Pepper and Sausage Bake

Mop up the juices with crusty rolls and serve a salad for a quick and really delicious supper.

6 green or red peppers	2 garlic cloves, chopped
12 small new potatoes	½ cup olive oil
1½ pounds hot or sweet Italian sausage	Salt and fresh pepper to taste

1. Cut the peppers into 4 pieces each. Remove the seeds and fibers.
2. Scrub the potatoes and dry.
3. Cut the sausage into 1½-inch chunks.
4. Arrange the peppers, potatoes, and sausage on a shallow baking dish. Sprinkle with the garlic. Drizzle the olive oil over. Mix with the hands or a large spoon to distribute the oil. Season with salt and pepper.
5. Bake in a 375-degree oven for 20 minutes, stirring occasionally. The potatoes should be tender when pierced with the tip of a small knife. Serves 4–6.

Sausage, Onion, and Mushroom Custard

½ pound sweet or hot Italian sausage, casings removed	½ cup freshly grated Parmesan cheese
4 tablespoons butter	Salt and fresh pepper to taste
½ pound mushrooms, sliced	2 eggs
1 pound yellow onions, chopped	2 egg yolks
	1 cup light cream

1. Crumble the sausage and cook it in its own fat in a 10-inch skillet until brown, 3–5 minutes. Remove with a slotted spoon to drain on paper towels.
2. Pour off the fat from the pan. Add 2 tablespoons of the butter. Add the mushrooms and toss over a high heat for 2–3 minutes. Remove to a bowl.
3. Add the remaining butter to the pan and cook the onions until limp, 5 minutes or longer.

4. Combine the sausage, mushrooms, and onions in a bowl. Add the cheese, salt, and pepper.
5. Beat together in a bowl the eggs and egg yolks and whisk in the cream. Pour over the sausage mixture, mix well, and fill a 9-inch shallow casserole with the mixture. Bake at 350 degrees until set, about 20 minutes. Serves 6.

Grilled or Broiled Italian Sausage

A toothpick stuck through a sausage will keep it from splitting.

1 pound hot Italian sausage
1 pound sweet Italian sausage

Red wine to cover sausage

1. Prick the sausages with the tip of a skewer in several places. Place in a pan and cover with wine. Bring to a boil. Cook 5 minutes to remove excess fat. Remove and drain. Dry thoroughly.
2. Place the sausages on a grill over hot coals and grill until brown, turning frequently, about 10 minutes. Or place on a broiler rack and broil 2 inches from the heating element for 10 minutes, turning frequently. Serve with crusty bread. Serves 6.

Variation

Roasted sausage: Place the sausages in a pan with ½ cup red wine. Bake in a 375-degree oven for 30 minutes, basting with the pan juices.

Salami Fritters

1 cup flour	1 cup chopped
1 teaspoon baking	mushrooms
powder	½ cup chopped ham
Salt and fresh pepper	1 egg white, stiffly
½ cup milk	beaten
2 eggs, beaten slightly	Oil for deep frying
1 cup chopped salami	

1. Combine the flour, baking powder, salt and pepper in
   a bowl. Stir in the milk and beaten eggs (batter will be
   lumpy).
2. Add the salami, mushrooms, and ham. Fold in the egg
   white.
3. Drop by tablespoonfuls into hot fat (375 degrees). Fry
   about 2 minutes, or until golden brown. Remove with
   a slotted spoon. Drain on paper towels. Makes about
   30 fritters.

Calf's Liver, Venice Style

I have had this dish in every restaurant in Venice. The
one I like best, however, is this one cooked by my friend
Clara Cassetti.

2½ pounds calf's liver	Salt and fresh pepper
¼ cup flour	to taste
6 tablespoons butter	¼ cup red wine vinegar
2 large onions, peeled	2 tablespoons chopped
and thinly sliced	flat-leaf parsley

1. Cut the liver into strips the size of an index finger.
   Dredge in flour. Set aside.
2. In a large skillet, heat 4 tablespoons of the butter.
   When the foam subsides, add the onions. Lower the
   heat and cook, while stirring, until the onions are very

soft, 10–15 minutes. Remove the onions and keep warm.

3. Heat the remaining 2 tablespoons butter in a skillet. When the foam subsides, add the liver strips. Stir them and allow to brown evenly.

4. Put the onions back in the pan and mix well with the liver. Season with salt and pepper. Add the vinegar. Raise the heat, stir to combine, add the parsley, and serve. Serves 4–6.

Liver with Herbs

8 tablespoons butter
1½ pounds calf's liver,
  thickly sliced
1 tablespoon chopped
  flat-leaf parsley

3–4 basil leaves,
  chopped
Juice of ½ lemon
Salt and fresh
  pepper to taste

1. Melt 4 tablespoons of the butter. When the foam subsides, add the liver and cook until brown on both sides, 2–3 minutes a side. The liver should be pink in the center. Remove to a serving platter.

2. Add the remaining butter to the pan. When hot, add the parsley, basil, and lemon juice. Swirl over heat 30 seconds. Pour over the liver. Season with salt and pepper. Serves 4–6.

Baby Lamb Chops with Gremolata

12 baby lamb chops
2 tablespoons butter,
  melted
  Salt and fresh pepper
  to taste
  Grated peel of 1
  lemon

2 garlic cloves, finely
  chopped
¼ cup finely chopped
  flat-leaf parsley

1. Brush the lamb chops with melted butter on both sides and sprinkle with salt and pepper.
2. Mix the remaining ingredients in a bowl.
3. Place the lamb chops on a broiler pan and set 3 inches from the broiler unit Broil 2 to 3 minutes on each side, or longer for better done chops. Scatter the gremolata mixture over the chops and serve. Serves 4.

Note: Add 1 tablespoon finely chopped fresh rosemary for a variation on the gremolata. Serve over lamb, broiled chicken, veal, or fish.

Breaded Lamb

2 cups fresh bread crumbs
8 tablespoons chopped flat-leaf parsley
4 garlic cloves, chopped
2 teaspoons chopped fresh rosemary

Salt and fresh pepper to taste
3½ pounds shoulder of lamb, cut into 1-inch cubes
⅓ cup olive oil

1. Mix together in a bowl the bread crumbs, parsley, garlic, rosemary, salt, and pepper.
2. Roll the lamb cubes in oil and then in the bread crumb mixture. Lay the cubes in a baking dish. Sprinkle any remaining oil over the meat.
3. Bake at 350 degrees for 30 minutes, until meat is tender and golden brown. Serves 4–6.

Variation

Substitute veal for lamb.

Chicken Breasts With Sausage

3 whole chicken breasts, skinned, boned, and halved	1 tablespoon chopped flat-leaf parsley
2 tablespoons oil	1 teaspoon chopped rosemary
1 small onion, chopped	Salt and fresh pepper to taste
1 garlic clove, chopped	
½ pound sweet Italian sausage, casings removed	4 tablespoons butter
	6 finger-size pieces mozzarella or Fontina
¾ cup fresh bread crumbs	¾ cup dry white wine
	Juice of ½ lemon

1. Flatten the 6 pieces of chicken by pounding with a wet mallet or pound between sheets of wax paper or foil.
2. Heat the oil in a skillet. When hot, add the onion, garlic, and sausage meat. Cook, while stirring with a wooden spatula, for about 5 minutes, or until the sausage is cooked through. Using a slotted spoon, remove the mixture to a bowl. Pour off the fat.
3. Mix the bread crumbs, parsley, and rosemary with the sausage. Season with salt and pepper. Melt the butter in the same skillet. When the foam subsides, sauté the chicken pieces, a few at a time, about 2 minutes a side.
4. Remove the chicken pieces. Lay them on a board or countertop and divide the filling evenly. Lay cheese on each. Roll up the chicken, tucking in the edges. Tie to secure or fasten with toothpicks. Lay in a baking dish, seam side down.
5. Add the wine and lemon juice to the skillet. Boil up to deglaze. Swirl around over heat for 1–2 minutes. Pour over the chicken. Bake at 350 degrees for 15–20 minutes. Remove strings or toothpicks. Serves 6.

Chicken Strips with Sage

3 whole chicken
   breasts, skinned and
   boned
¾ cup flour
4 tablespoons butter
   Salt and fresh pepper
   to taste

1–2 sage leaves,
   chopped
½ cup red wine
1 tablespoon chopped
   flat-leaf parsley

1. Cut the chicken breasts into finger strips. Roll them in flour.
2. Melt the butter in a skillet. When the foam subsides, add the chicken strips, salt, pepper, and sage. Cook 5 minutes, or until the chicken is no longer pink. Stir occasionally.
3. Add the red wine and cook 2–3 minutes, scraping and stirring. Add the chopped parsley and serve. Serves 4–6.

Variation

Chicken Strips with Butter and Lemon. Sauté the chicken strips as above. Substitute the juice of 1 lemon and 2 more tablespoons butter for the sage and wine.

Chicken Rolls with Ham and Cheese

3 whole chicken breasts,
   skinned and boned
4 tablespoons butter
6 thin slices prosciutto
1–2 sage leaves,
   chopped

6 thin slices Fontina
   cheese
4 tablespoons butter
½ cup dry white wine

1. Cut the chicken in half lengthwise. Pound to flatten with a wet mallet or pound between sheets of wax paper or foil.
2. Melt 4 tablespoons butter in a skillet. Sauté the chicken breasts in the hot butter for 2 minutes a side.
3. Lay the chicken on a board or countertop and place a slice of prosciutto on each piece. Sprinkle with a touch of sage (not too much). Top each with a slice of cheese. Roll up, tucking in the ends. Place in a baking dish.
4. Mix together the 4 tablespoons melted butter and wine and pour over the chicken. Bake at 350 degrees for 15–20 minutes. Serves 6.

Chicken Hunter's Style

2 tablespoons olive oil
4 tablespoons butter
1 chicken (3½ pounds), cut into pieces
¼ cup flour
  Salt and fresh pepper to taste
1 cup chopped celery
1 cup chopped onion
1–2 cup cloves, chopped
¼ pound mushrooms, sliced

3 tomatoes, peeled, seeded, and chopped
½ cup dry white wine
1 cup chicken stock
1 tablespoon tomato paste
2 tablespoons dry Marsala
2 tablespoons chopped flat-leaf parsley

1. Heat the oil and 2 tablespoons of the butter in a large skillet.
2. Roll the pieces of chicken in flour, shaking off excess. When the fat is hot, brown the chicken on high heat for 5 minutes on each side. The pieces will brown better if not touching. Season with salt and pepper.
3. In a sauté pan, heat the remaining 2 tablespoons butter. When the foam subsides add the celery and onion and cook until onion wilts.

4. Add the garlic and mushrooms and cook 1–2 minutes.
5. Add the tomatoes and cook 5 minutes.
6. Add the white wine, chicken stock, and tomato paste and cook until the sauce begins to reduce and thicken, about 8 minutes.
7. Meanwhile, remove the chicken from the skillet and place in the pan with the sauce. Pour off excess grease from the skillet, add the Marsala, and scrape up any brown bits. Add to the sauce. Simmer the chicken 15–20 minutes, or until tender. Place the chicken on a serving dish and spoon the sauce over. Garnish with parsley. Serves 4–6.

Gloria's Chicken with Bay Leaves

Gloria Etting is one of my favorite Italians. She is also one of my favorite Italian cooks.

4 tablespoons olive oil
4 tablespoons butter
2 chickens (3½ pounds each), cut into pieces
¼ cup finely chopped onion
1½ pounds mushrooms, stems chopped, caps halved

6 bay leaves
Juice of 2 lemons
Salt and fresh pepper to taste
½ cup chopped flat-leaf parsley
¾ cup chicken stock

1. Heat the oil and butter in a large skillet. When hot, add the chicken, a few pieces at a time, and brown on both sides. When all the chicken is brown, set aside.

2. Add the onion and chopped mushroom stems to the pan. If there are chicken livers, cut them up and add them. Stir in the bay leaves, lemon juice, salt, and pepper. Add half the parsley and ¾ cup chicken stock.
3. Put the chicken back in the pan and cover. Simmer the chicken 20 minutes or more until tender. Add the mushroom caps the last 10 minutes.
4. Arrange the chicken on a platter. Reduce the juices. Remove the bay leaves and pour the sauce over the chicken. Garnish with remaining parsley. Serves 8.

Chicken Mario

4 tablespoons olive oil
1 chicken (3½ pounds), cut up
  Salt and fresh pepper to taste
1 medium onion, chopped

1 garlic clove, chopped
2 sage leaves
  Few sprigs rosemary
¾ cup dry white wine
½ cup chicken stock
2 tomatoes, peeled, seeded, and chopped

1. Heat the oil in a large skillet. Add the chicken and brown 5 minutes on each side. Do not crowd the pan. Season with salt and pepper.
2. Add the onion, garlic, sage leaves, and rosemary. Pour the wine and stock over and bring to a boil. Scatter the tomatoes over. Cover and cook 20 minutes. Remove the lid and cook on high heat 5 minutes to reduce the juices. Serves 4–6.

Deviled Chicken

12 tablespoons butter
½ cup olive oil
1 teaspoon red pepper
  flakes, or to taste
1 large onion, chopped
2 garlic cloves, chopped
2 chickens (2½ to 3
  pounds), halved or
  quartered, or the
  equivalent of pieces
  such as legs, thighs,
  or breasts

Salt to taste
Juice of 1 lemon
½ cup of fresh bread
  crumbs
Parsley sprigs for
  garnish
Lemon quarters for
  garnish

1. Melt the butter in a small saucepan. Add 4 tablespoons of the oil, pepper flakes, onion, and garlic.
2. Rub the chicken with the remaining oil, salt and lemon juice. Place on a broiler rack, skin side down, 4 inches from the heating element. Broil 5–7 minutes. Baste with the butter mixture. Turn the chicken skin side up and continue to broil 15–20 minutes longer. Baste occasionally with the butter mixture.
3. Sprinkle the chicken with the bread crumbs and remaining butter mixture and broil 5 minutes more. Serve with parsley and lemon quarters. Serves 6–8.

Batter-Fried Chicken

Oil for deep frying
1 cup flour
1 teaspoon baking
  powder
1 teaspoon salt
2 eggs
⅔ cup milk
2 tablespoons butter,
  melted

1½ cups dry bread
  crumbs
⅓ cup freshly grated
  Parmesan cheese
3 whole chicken
  breasts, boned,
  skinned, and cut
  into quarters
Lemon wedges

1. Heat the oil to 350–360 degrees.
2. Mix together the flour, baking powder, and salt in a bowl.
3. Beat the eggs until thick. Add the milk and melted butter. Beat in the flour mixture gradually. The batter will be slightly lumpy.
4. In another bowl, mix together the bread crumbs and Parmesan cheese. Dip the chicken pieces into the batter and then into crumbs. Place the pieces on a baking sheet.
5. Drop 4 or 5 pieces of chicken at a time into the hot fat. Allow 8–10 minutes for cooking chicken, depending on size. When the chicken is almost cooked, the pieces will rise to the surface of the fat.
6. Remove the chicken pieces with a slotted spoon. Drain on brown paper. Serve with lemon wedges. Serves 4–6.

Roast Chicken with Rosemary

2 roasting chickens (3½
   to 4 pounds each)
1 lemon, cut in half
4 tablespoons olive oil
Salt and fresh
   pepper to taste

4 tablespoons butter
1 long branch
   rosemary, 4–5
   inches, cut in two

1. Rub the chickens all over with lemon. Put the squeezed lemon halves in the cavities of the birds. Rub the chickens with olive oil, salt, and pepper. Put 2 tablespoons butter in each cavity. Place a piece of rosemary branch on top of each chicken. Truss the chickens if you prefer, but it is not necessary. Place on a rack in a roasting pan.

2. Roast at 375 degrees for 1 hour, basting with the pan juices from time to time. Turn the chicken from side to side every 15 minutes.
3. Degrease the pan juices. Carve the chicken and serve with the juices. Serves 6–8.

Turkey Breast with Wine

Turkey breast may be replacing chicken as the workhorse of the American kitchen. It can be used in any dish that calls for veal, and it looks better, tastes better, and has more texture than chicken breast. And it doesn't cost an arm and a leg.

4 tablespoons butter, or more

2–3 pounds turkey breast, sliced and pounded to ¼ inch thick (12 slices for 6 servings)

¾ cup flour

Salt and fresh pepper to taste

1 cup dry white wine
Grated rind and juice of 1 lemon

2 tablespoons chopped flat-leaf parsley

1. Heat the butter in a large sauté pan.
2. Roll the turkey pieces in flour and pat off excess. When the butter foam subsides, add the turkey slices, a few at a time. Do not let them touch. Add butter as necessary to cook 12 slices. Cook them for 2 minutes on each side. Add salt and pepper. Remove the turkey to a serving dish.
3. Add the wine and lemon juice to the pan juices. Bring to a boil, scraping up any brown bits in the pan. Cook on high heat 3–5 minutes to reduce. Add the grated lemon rind. Pour the mixture over the turkey. Garnish with parsley. Serves 6.

Variations

¾ cup freshly grated
   Parmesan

Turkey breast with Parmesan cheese. Sauté the turkey
slices as above. Lay on a broiler pan. Sprinkle each slice
with Parmesan cheese, ¾ cup in all. Broil 2–3 minutes,
2 inches from the heating element. Serve as is or with
wine-lemon sauce as above.

12 thin slices Fontina
   cheese
	12 thin slices truffle,
	   white or black
	   (optional)

Turkey breast with Fontina cheese and truffle. Sauté
the turkey slices as above. Lay on a baking pan. Lay a
slice of Fontina cheese on each turkey slice. Put a slice
of truffle on each. Place in a 375-degree oven for 2–3
minutes, until the cheese is melted. If the truffle is omit-
ted, serve the turkey with the wine-lemon sauce as above.

½ cup dry white wine
4–5 basil leaves,
   chopped
	1 cup heavy cream
	Salt and fresh pepper
	   to taste

Turkey breast with basil cream sauce. Sauté the turkey
slices as above. Remove to a serving dish. Add the wine
and basil to the pan and cook 1 minute. Add the heavy
cream. Boil gently to thicken the cream, 3–5 minutes,
until it coats the back of a spoon. Season with salt and
pepper and pour over turkey.

2 tablespoons butter
½ pound mushrooms,
   thinly sliced
Juice of ½ lemon
Salt and fresh pepper
   to taste
	2 tablespoons dry
	   Marsala
	1 cup heavy cream

Turkey breast with mushroom cream sauce. Sauté the turkey slices as above. Melt the butter in a skillet. When the foam subsides, add the mushrooms, lemon juice, salt, and pepper. Toss over heat for 3 minutes. Add the Marsala and reduce over high heat. Add the heavy cream and cook until the cream thickens and coats the back of a metal spoon, 3–5 minutes. Pour over turkey.

Turkey pillows or sandwiches. Sauté the turkey slices as above. Arrange a truffle slice and a slice of Fontina cheese on each. Fold over as for a turnover. Or top with another turkey slice. Pinch the edges together and bake at 375 degrees until the cheese melts, 2–3 minutes.

Cornish Hens in Marsala

6 Cornish hens (1 pound each)	1 cup dry Marsala
6 sage leaves	1 cup chicken stock
8 tablespoons butter, softened	Parsley
	Lemon wedges
Salt and fresh pepper to taste	

1. Wash and dry the hens. Place 1 sage leaf in the cavity of each. Rub the hens with butter and season with salt and pepper.
2. Place the hens in a shallow roasting pan. Add the Marsala and half the stock. Bake at 375 degrees until tender, about 45 minutes. Test after 35 minutes by pricking a leg. If the juices run clear, the birds are done. Baste occasionally while roasting. Remove the birds to a platter.
3. Remove the grease from the pan juices. Add the rest of the stock. Bring to a boil. Cook 2–3 minutes to

reduce a little and to intensify the flavor, and pour over the birds. Serve with a bunch of flat-leaf parsley and lemon wedges. Serves 6.

Variation

The hens can be baked with dry vermouth in place of Marsala.

Roasted Squabs with Sage Butter

12 tablespoons butter
 6 fresh sage leaves
 6 squabs, cleaned and
    oven ready

Salt and fresh pepper to taste

1. Melt the butter in a skillet. Add the sage leaves. Cook until the butter begins to brown. Remove the sage leaves.
2. Rub the squabs with a little of the butter. Place them on a rack, breast side up, in a roasting pan. Season with salt and pepper. Place in a 425-degree oven and roast 25–30 minutes, depending on desired doneness. Baste the birds with the sage butter two or three times during the roasting time. Pour any remaining butter over the birds and serve. Serves 6.

Chicken Livers with Sage

Chicken livers go in and out of style—for some reason I can't figure out. They are high in protein, low in fat, and take nicely to a wide variety of flavors. Sage provides an interesting tang in this recipe; just remember that sage is an extremely strong herb so don't use too much.

4 tablespoons butter
1½ pounds chicken
livers, cleaned and
dried

1–2 fresh sage leaves,
chopped

Salt and fresh
pepper to taste
¼ cup dry Marsala

1. Heat the butter in a skillet. When the foam subsides, add the livers. Cook 3 minutes over high heat. Do not touch them. After 3 minutes, turn them over, add the sage, and cook 2–3 minutes. The edges should be brown and crisp. Remove the livers to a serving dish. Season with salt and pepper.

2. Add the Marsala to the pan. Reduce the heat and stir to deglaze. Swirl the pan on heat for 1–2 minutes. Pour over the livers. Serves 4–6.

10

FRUITS AND DESSERTS

IN ITALY, DESSERT USUALLY MEANS FRUIT. SOMETHING as simple as a bowl of cherries brought to the table with a bowl of ice water on the side, so you can dip each cherry to clean and cool it before you pop it in your mouth.

Or strawberries marinated briefly with a few drops of vinegar on each serving, which brings out the sweetness.

Or peach or pear flowers—which I love, and which I suspect makes the waiters in Italian restaurants dislike me, especially on busy nights. Because I always ask them to do it. The waiter takes a peach and peels it completely in one long continuous ribbon, cuts the peach into tiny wedges, arranges it like a flower on a plate, then takes another peach and does the same thing, overlapping all the little petals. When both white and yellow peaches are available, they use both, making a big beautiful chrysanthemum on the plate.

You can do this at home if you know how. Otherwise, serve the fruit straight up; it tastes just as good, even if it doesn't look nearly as beautiful.

Mixed Fruit

When people ask me what dessert I served last night, most of the time I answer, "mixed fruit." This is one of the quickest, easiest, and one of the very best desserts I know of.

Sliced oranges, or sections	Black and green grapes
Sliced grapefruit, or sections	Sliced pears
Sliced bananas	Sliced apples
	Strawberries, blueberries or whatever is in season

Into a large bowl, put all or a combination of the fruits. Sprinkle with sugar and brandy to taste. Mix well. Chill.

Cantaloupe with Fruit

3 small ripe cantaloupes	2 tablespoons orange juice
3 cups fresh strawberries	1 tablespoon lemon juice
2 cups fresh raspberries	
½ cup sweet Marsala	
2 tablespoons sugar	

1. Cut the melons in half and remove the seeds.
2. Hull and wash the berries and drain. Combine the berries with wine, sugar, and juices and fill the cavities of the melons. Chill before serving. Serves 6.

Caramelized Cherries

Not as crunchy as candied apples, but just as bright and shiny, and they make a great dessert.

8 tablespoons butter
2 pounds Bing cherries,
stems and pits
removed

⅔ cup sugar
4 tablespoons kirsch

1. Melt the butter in a large skillet. When very hot, add the cherries. Cook, while stirring with a wooden spatula, for 3–5 minutes, or until the cherries release some of their juice.
2. Add the sugar and continue to stir until the sugar caramelizes slightly, about 3 minutes.
3. Add the kirsch, tilt the pan so the liqueur flames, or ignite with a match. Serves 6–8.

Bananas Baked in Marsala

4 tablespoons flour
½ cup sugar
½ teaspoon cinnamon
Freshly grated
nutmeg to taste
6–8 bananas, peeled
and cut lengthwise

6 tablespoons butter,
melted
½ cup sweet Marsala
1 cup heavy cream

1. Mix together the flour, sugar, cinnamon, and nutmeg. Roll the bananas in this mixture.
2. Place the bananas close together in a baking dish. Pour the butter over and add Marsala to the dish. Bake at 350 degrees until the bananas are golden, approximately 20 minutes.
3. Serve the bananas from the dish. Spoon some of the sauce over each serving and drizzle with a bit of heavy cream. Serves 4–6.

Cherries in Chianti

2½ pounds sour cherries, pitted and stemmed	2–3 cups Chianti
	1 teaspoon cinnamon
1 cup sugar	2 cups heavy cream, whipped lightly

1. In a saucepan, combine the cherries, sugar, wine, and cinnamon. Bring to a boil, turn to simmer, and cook for 15–30 minutes, or until the cherries are very soft.
2. Stir over ice to cool. Serve in a large bowl with whipped cream on the side. Serves 6.

Figs in Cocoa

A quick recipe that combines surprising flavors and looks just as good as it tastes. From my friend Fernanda Gosetti of Milan.

12 ripe figs, peeled	2 tablespoons confectioners' sugar
1 cup ricotta cheese	
¼ cup heavy cream	Cocoa
2 tablespoons orange liqueur	

1. Cut the figs twice through the center but do not cut through the base. Stand them on a serving platter. Spread them open.
2. Place the ricotta in a bowl and thin with the cream. Add the orange liqueur and sugar. Spoon the mixture neatly over the figs. Dust each fig with a tiny bit of cocoa. Chill 15 minutes. Serves 4–6.

Fresh Figs in Wine

12–16 fresh figs, peeled
¼ cup
    confectioners'
    sugar
½ teaspoon
    cinnamon

2 tablespoons brandy
4 tablespoons sweet
    Marsala
Pitcher of heavy cream

Place the figs in layers in a bowl. Dust with sugar and cinnamon. Sprinkle with brandy and add the Marsala. Toss to blend the flavors. Serve with heavy cream. Serves 4–6.

Note: These figs are even better if allowed to chill for 1–2 hours.

Grapes with Vanilla Sauce

3 cups green seedless
    grapes
2 cups red seedless
    grapes (if available),
    otherwise seed the
    grapes

VANILLA SAUCE

2 cups milk
3 egg yolks
1 whole egg
½ cup sugar
2–3 teaspoons good
    vanilla, or to taste

1. Remove the stems and wash grapes. Mix together and place in a decorative glass bowl. Chill.
2. Bring the milk to the scalding point.
3. Whisk the egg yolks, egg, and sugar until thick. Add the hot milk slowly, whisking into the eggs and sugar.
4. Return to the saucepan and stir or whisk over heat until the sauce is slightly thickened and will coat the back of a metal spoon.

5. Remove from the heat and stir in the vanilla. Pour over
   chilled grapes. Serves 4–6.

Note: The sauce may be chilled before pouring over the
grapes. Chill in the refrigerator or stir over ice. This custard sauce may be used on cake or other fruit.

Nectarines with Champagne

8–10 nectarines, peeled   1 split Asti spumante
    and sliced
    2 tablespoons
    maraschino
    liqueur

Put the nectarines in a bowl. Add the liqueur. Just
before serving, pour Asti spumante over the nectarines.
Serves 4–6.

Baked Fresh Peaches

6 large peaches, cut in   2 tablespoons butter,
    half, pits removed   melted
    Juice of 1 lemon   1 egg yolk
1 cup crushed   2 tablespoons sweet
    macaroons   Marsala, or more
2 tablespoons sugar   Few slivered almonds

1. Butter a baking dish large enough to hold 12 peach
   halves. Lay the unpeeled peach halves cut side up in
   the baking dish. Using a melon baller, enlarge the cavity in each peach.
2. Put the scooped-out pieces of fruit in a bowl with the
   lemon juice. Add the macaroons, sugar, butter, and
   egg yolk. Crush with a fork and mix to blend. Moisten
   with Marsala, enough to make a paste of the mixture.

3. Divide the mixture among the 12 peach halves. Sprinkle each half with a few almond slivers. Place in a 375-degree oven and bake 25–30 minutes. Check for doneness after 20 minutes. Serve warm or cold, with or without heavy cream. Serves 6.

Peach and Plum Compote

This is nothing more than fruit in sugar syrup. It is a great way to turn green or out of season fruit into something that will remind you of the height of summer. And in the height of summer, it is a great way to glorify fruit that is already ripe.

1 cup sugar
1 cup water
  Juice and rind of ½
  lemon
Juice of 1 orange

Stick cinnamon
5 peaches, peeled and
  pits removed
6 plums

1. Place the sugar in a saucepan with the water, lemon rind and juice, orange juice, and cinnamon. Bring to a boil, stirring. Boil 5 minutes, or until the mixture is syrupy.
2. Slice the peaches and add to the syrup. Cover and simmer 2–3 minutes. Remove the peaches with a slotted spoon and place in a serving dish.
3. Prick the plums in several places and add to the syrup. Cover and simmer 5 minutes. Remove the plums to the serving bowl.
4. Simmer the syrup a few minutes, uncovered. Remove the cinnamon and pour over fruit. Chill before serving or stir over ice to cool rapidly. Serves 4–6.

Fresh Peaches with Prosecco

The most popular Prosecco wine is a light spumante, naturally fermented. Any sparkling white wine could be substituted.

6 ripe peaches　　　　　*Juice of ½ lemon*
½ cup sugar　　　　　　*1 bottle Prosecco*

1. Drop the peaches into a kettle of boiling water for 10 seconds. Remove with a slotted spoon and, when cool enough to handle, peel carefully. Leave whole. Place in a bowl and sprinkle with the sugar and lemon juice. Chill during dinner.
2. Just before serving, pour the Prosecco over the peaches and serve in large wine glasses. Serves 6.

Peaches in Marsala

Pears are equally good here.

6 ripe peaches　　　　　*1 cup heavy cream,*
2 cups sugar　　　　　　　*whipped*
2 cups sweet Marsala
* Grated peel and juice*
* of 2 lemons*

1. Drop the peaches into a kettle of boiling water for 10 seconds. Remove with a slotted spoon. When cool enough to handle, remove the skin. Leave them whole and place them in a shallow baking dish, approximately 8 inches square.
2. Bring the sugar, wine, lemon peel, and juice to a boil over medium heat. Pour over the peaches.
3. Cover the peaches with a tent of aluminum foil. Bake in a 400-degree oven for 20–30 minutes, or until tender.

Baste two or three times during cooking. Serve warm with whipped cream. Serves 6.

Pears Stuffed with Gorgonzola Cheese

There is nothing more satisfying than eating a luscious ripe pear with some creamy Gorgonzola cheese for dessert. For a fancier method of fixing, stuff the pear with the cheese.

6 ripe pears
3/4 pound Gorgonzola
  cheese

1/4 pound butter

1. Wash and dry the pears. Do not peel. Remove the cores with an apple corer from the bottom of the pears. Leave stems on. Cut a slice off the bottom of each pear so it will stand upright on a serving dish.
2. Beat the cheese and butter together until creamy in a mixer or food processor. Put the mixture in a pastry bag fitted with a star tube. Pipe the mixture into each pear cavity.
3. Stand the pears on individual serving dishes and pipe a few stars around the base of each pear. Garnish with a shiny leaf. Serves 6.

Stuffed Pears

6 large firm ripe pears
  Lemon juice with a
  little water
3/4 cup confectioners'
  sugar
1/2 cup toasted almonds,
  ground

4 candied cherries,
  chopped fine
1/4 teaspoon almond
  extract
1/2 cup dry Marsala

1. Wash the pears, cut in half, and peel. With a melon ball cutter, scoop out the cores. Place in lemon juice to keep from discoloring. Lay the pears in a low shallow baking dish.
2. Blend together the confectioners' sugar, ground almonds, chopped cherries, and almond extract. Fill the cavities of the pears with the mixture. Pour the Marsala over the pears and baste a few times.
3. Cover the dish and bake for 15 minutes at 350 degrees. Remove the cover and bake until fork tender, about 10 minutes. Baste a couple of times during the baking period. Serve very hot or cold. Serves 6–8.

Candied Fruits

4½ cups sugar	Pinch cream of tartar
1 cup water	Black and green grapes
2 tablespoons light corn syrup	Tangerine sections
	Strawberries

1. Bring the sugar, water, corn syrup, and cream of tartar to a boil. Using a candy thermometer, boil to 300–320 degrees. Remove the pan from the heat and set in a pan of lukewarm water.
2. Using a toothpick or tweezers, dip the fruit, one piece at a time, into the syrup. Place the fruit on a greased marble slab or baking sheet. Serve as soon as possible. Makes enough syrup for 24 pieces of fruit.

Italian Macaroons

2 cups blanched almonds	1 teaspoon almond extract
2 egg whites	½ cup confectioners' sugar
1 cup granulated sugar	

1. Grind the almonds in a blender or food processor. Spread them on a baking sheet and place in a 300-degree oven for 10 minutes to dry out.
2. Beat the egg whites until stiff but not dry. Put into a bowl with the nuts, granulated sugar, and almond extract. Blend together gently.
3. Drop by teaspoonfuls 2 inches apart onto a parchment-lined baking sheet. Sprinkle with confectioners' sugar. Bake at 325 degrees for 15–20 minutes until light brown. Makes about 2 dozen.

Florentines

1 cup blanched, slivered almonds
½ cup heavy cream
3 tablespoons sugar
½ pound candied orange peel, finely chopped
¼ cup flour
2 ounces semi-sweet chocolate

1. Toast the almonds in a 350-degree oven for 10–15 minutes.
2. Stir the cream and sugar together in a bowl and add the orange peel, almonds, and flour.
3. Line two baking sheets with parchment. Drop the batter onto the parchment by teaspoonfuls about 2 inches apart. Bake at 350 degrees for 30–35 minutes. Watch them closely, as they burn easily.
4. Remove from the oven. Lift the cookies off the pan with a spatula and place on racks to cool. When cold, brush the bottoms of the cookies with melted chocolate. The chocolate will set in 5 minutes. Makes about 2½ dozen.

Pine Nut Cookies

½ pound almond paste   ¼ pound pine nuts
1 cup sugar
2 lightly beaten egg
   whites

1. Put the almond paste and sugar in a mixer bowl or food processor. Beat to mix thoroughly. Add the egg whites and beat until well blended.
2. With wet hands, form the dough, 1 teaspoon at a time, into crescents. Dip the tops of the cookies into pine nuts and place on a baking sheet lined with parchment or brown paper.
3. Bake at 350 degrees for 15 minutes. Cool completely before removing from the sheet. Makes about 24.

Cookie Slices with Anise

5 eggs
½ cup sugar, plus sugar
   for sprinkling on
   dough
6 drops anise extract
4 cups flour, measured
   lightly
1 teaspoon baking
   powder
½ teaspoon baking
   powder

½ teaspoon salt
½ cup light raisins,
   chopped
½ cup blanched
   almonds, chopped
⅓ cup finely chopped
   citron
½ pound butter,
   softened
1 egg, beaten

1. Beat the 5 eggs in a large mixing bowl until thick. Add the ½ cup sugar, mixing well. Add the anise, flour, baking powder, salt, raisins, almonds, and citron. Add the softened butter. If it becomes too thick for the mixer, remove to a lightly floured board. Knead the dough until smooth and manageable.

2. Divide the dough in half and roll each into oblong pieces 3 inches wide and about ¾ inch thick. Brush with beaten egg. Sprinkle with sugar. Cut into 1-inch slices.

3. Place on greased cookie sheets. Bake at 350 degrees 20–25 minutes. Remove and cool on racks. Store in an airtight container. Makes 2½ dozen.

Note: Serve with wine or dunk in wine.

Chocolate Almonds

2 cups unblanched whole almonds

2 cups semi-sweet chocolate bits, melted

1. Place the almonds on a baking sheet. Bake in a 350-degree oven for 10–15 minutes until crisp. Watch carefully to prevent them from burning. Cool.

2. Place the almonds in a bowl with the melted chocolate and mix well. Place each coated almond on a baking sheet lined with foil or wax paper. Chill until chocolate sets. Makes 2 cups.

Chocolate Truffles

Good with a hot cup of rich espresso coffee.

1 pound dark sweet chocolate
1 cup heavy cream

30 candied cherries
Cocoa

1. Break up the chocolate and melt it with the heavy cream. Do this slowly and stir. Do not boil.

2. Pour onto a shallow baking sheet and place in the freezer for 15–20 minutes until the mixture sets.

3. Remove a spoonful of chocolate at a time and roll around a cherry. Roll in cocoa and place on a platter. Chill before serving. Makes 30 or more.

Chestnut Dessert

1 can (15 ounces)
sweetened chestnut
purée
½ pound unsalted butter
Confectioners' sugar
2 tablespoons Marsala

½ cup toasted pine nuts
1 cup heavy cream,
whipped
Whole candied
chestnuts

1. In a mixer bowl, beat the chestnut purée and the butter until very smooth, light, and creamy.
2. Add sugar to taste. Add the wine and pine nuts. Combine well. Place in a very small dessert dishes or soufflé pots or in a large serving bowl.
3. Add 2 tablespoons confectioners' sugar to the whipped cream. Place in a pastry bag fitted with a star tube. Pipe rosettes on top of the dessert. Garnish with candied chestnuts. Chill. Serves 8–12.

Pizzelles

You need an iron that gives the cookies a ridged pattern on the surface for these.

3 eggs
¾ cup sugar
8 tablespoons butter,
melted

1 tablespoon anisette
1 teaspoon vanilla
1½ cups flour (lightly
measured)

1. Beat the eggs in a small mixer bowl until lemon colored and stiff. Add the sugar gradually. Add the cool melted butter until well blended. Add the anisette and vanilla.
2. Change the batter to a larger mixer bowl and gradually add the flour. Beat until well mixed.
3. Follow the manufacturer's directions for using a pizzelle iron. Makes 28–30 small, or 18–2 large, cookies.

Variation

Use lemon juice and grated lemon rind instead of anisette, or a combination of lemon and orange juice and
rind.

Anna's Siena Cake

1 cup almonds
1 cup hazelnuts
3 ounces candied
  orange rind
2 tablespoons cocoa
1/3 cup flour
2 teaspoons cinnamon
1/2 teaspoon allspice

1 teaspoon vanilla
  extract
Pinch of salt
1/2 cup sugar
1/2 cup honey
Confectioners' sugar

1. Coarsely chop the nuts. Put into a large mixing bowl.
2. Chop the candied lemon and orange rind and add. Add
   the cocoa, flour, cinnamon, allspice, vanilla, and salt.
   Blend thoroughly.
2. Bring the sugar and honey to a boil and cook to the
   soft ball stage, 238 degrees. Pour into the bowl and
   blend well.
4. Line a round 9-inch cake pan with parchment. Press
   the mixture evenly into the pan. Bake in a 300-degree
   oven for 30 minutes.
5. Sift confectioners' sugar thickly over the top while
   still hot. Let cool in the pan. Wrap in foil and keep
   in a cool place. Keeps well for a couple of months.
   Serves 6.

Ricotta with Coffee

1½ pounds ricotta
  cheese
2 tablespoons finely
  ground espresso
  coffee

½ cup sugar
3 tablespoons rum

Put the ricotta through the finest blade of a food mill. Add the coffee, sugar, and rum and mix well. Pour into a serving dish and chill by placing in the freezer for ½ hour or so. Serves 4–6.

Creamy Ricotta Dessert

3½ cups ricotta cheese
  ¼ cup flour
    Salt (optional)
    Grated rind of 1
    lemon

    Grated rind of 1
    orange
1 teaspoon vanilla
4 eggs, beaten
1 cup sugar

1. Butter a 1½-quart baking dish.
2. Put all the ingredients in a bowl and mix with a wooden spatula until well blended.
3. Scrape into the prepared baking dish and bake in a 350-degree oven for 45 minutes to 1 hour, or until firm. Serve warm or chilled. Serves 6–8.

Ricotta Cake

5 eggs, separated
¾ cup sugar
⅓ cup finely chopped
  candied orange peel
  Grated rind of 1
  lemon

1 cup ground blanched
  almonds
1 pound ricotta cheese,
  strained and put
  through the fine blade
  of a food mill

1. Preheat the oven to 325 degrees.
2. Grease and flour a 9-inch glass pie plate.
3. Beat the egg yolks on high speed in a small mixer bowl until lemon colored and thick. Continue beating, gradually adding sugar, until well mixed. Add the orange peel, lemon rind, and ground almonds. Remove the bowl from the mixer and fold in the ricotta cheese.
4. Beat the egg whites with clean beaters in a larger mixer bowl until stiff but not dry. Quickly fold the egg yolk mixture into the egg whites, a little at a time.
5. Pour into the prepared pie plate. Bake at 325 degrees for 45–50 minutes. Serves 8–12.

Variation

Substitute chocolate pieces for the candied fruit.

Zabaglione

True zabaglione contains only egg yolks. I always use a couple of whole eggs to lighten the mixture; otherwise I find it too heavy.

3 eggs
3 egg yolks
⅔ cup sugar

¼ cup sweet Marsala or any liqueur

1. Put the eggs, egg yolks, sugar, and Marsala into a zabaglione pot and beat with a whisk until blended. Hold the pot over high heat and continue beating; raise and lower the pot over the heat so that the pot never gets too hot. (Or put the ingredients into a large glass bowl, stand the bowl in a pan of hot water over high heat, and beat with whisk.)
2. When the zabaglione is thick and creamy (about 10 minutes over direct heat, 15 to 20 minutes over hot

water), serve immediately in stem glasses or pour over fresh fruit, such as strawberries, raspberries, sliced peaches. Serves 6.

Variations

To serve cold. Whip 1 cup heavy cream until peaks form. Set the warm zabaglione over a bowl of ice and beat until finger warm. Fold the whipped cream into the mixture.

To broil zabaglione with fruit. Make zabaglione with 6 egg yolks instead of 3, and substitute 3 tablespoons orange liqueur for the Marsala. Add 4 tablespoons orange juice and 2 tablespoons orange rind. Arrange peeled and halved peaches or peeled and sliced oranges in a flat baking dish. Pour the zabaglione over the fruit. Place 2 to 3 inches under a hot broiler. Watch carefully. Leave only long enough to scorch the top: just a few minutes.

Amaretto Soufflé

3 tablespoons butter	1–2 tablespoons
3 tablespoons flour	Amaretto liqueur
⅓ cup sugar	7 egg whites
1 cup milk	¼ teaspoon cream of
5 egg yolks	tartar
1 teaspoon vanilla	

1. Melt the butter in a small saucepan. Add the flour and stir with a wooden spatula to mix well. Don't let it brown.
2. Remove from the heat and add the sugar and milk. Switch to a whisk and return the pan to the heat. Whisk rapidly until the mixture comes to a boil and is smooth.
3. Set off the heat and rapidly whisk in the egg yolks. Add the vanilla and Amaretto.
4. Beat the egg whites with the cream of tartar in a mixer

or in a copper bowl until stiff but not dry. Gently fold into the yolk mixture.
5. Pour into a 6-cup soufflé dish and bake on the bottom shelf of a 375-degree oven for 30 minutes. Serves 4–6.

Variation

This soufflé can be poured into a 4-cup soufflé dish fitted with a collar. The dish may be buttered and sugared, if desired. For a bit of crunch, layer the soufflé mixture with crushed macaroons that have been soaked in Amaretto. Try Galliano, Strega or maraschino liqueur in place of Amaretto.

Amaretto Chocolate Sauce

½ cup cocoa	3 tablespoons butter
1 cup sugar	1 teaspoon vanilla
1 cup light corn syrup	1 tablespoon Amaretto,
½ cup light cream	or more to taste

1. Put all the ingredients except the vanilla and Amaretto into a small heavy pan. Slowly bring to a boil, stirring with a wooden spatula. Let boil 3 minutes only.
2. Remove from the heat and add the vanilla and Amaretto. Stir to incorporate the flavors. Serve over vanilla or coffee ice cream. Makes 2 cups.

Amaretto Cream

¾ cup crumbled Amaretti cookies	1½ pounds cream cheese
3–4 tablespoons espresso or strong coffee	½ cup sugar
	2 eggs
	1 teaspoon Amaretto liqueur

Place the cookies in a food processor to pulverize. Add the coffee, cheese, sugar, eggs, and liqueur. Process until creamy. Stop and scrape the sides of the bowl occasionally. Spoon into glasses and chill. Serves 4–6.

Vanilla Ice Cream

Italian ice cream is world famous. I'm convinced it's because the cream is better.

4 egg yolks	1½ inch piece vanilla
⅔ cup sugar	bean, scraped
3 cups milk, heated to	½ cup heavy cream
boiling point	

1. Combine the egg yolks and sugar in a bowl or mixer and whisk until thick. Gradually whisk in the hot milk.
2. Place in a nonaluminum saucepan and stir or whisk over medium heat until the mixture coats the back of a metal spoon; do not boil.
3. Remove from the heat and stir in the vanilla bean and heavy cream. Transfer the mixture to a bowl and set the bowl over ice. Stir the cream until it cools to room temperature. Freeze according to manufacturer's directions. Makes approximately 1 quart.

Variations

Amaretti ice cream. Add ¾ cup chopped Amaretti macaroons to partly frozen mixture.

Fruit ice cream. Omit the vanilla and mix in 2½ cups puréed fruit—peach, apricot, orange, papaya, pineapple, or banana. If using berries, puré them through a strainer to remove seeds. Add the juice of 1 lemon and 2 tablespoons liqueur to complement the fruit, if desired— framboise or kirsch for raspberry or strawberry, rum for pineapple and banana. Maraschino liqueur can be used in any of the fruit ice creams.

Chocolate Ice Cream

4 ounces dark sweet
  chocolate, broken
3 cups milk
²/₃ cup sugar

4 egg yolks
1½ inch piece vanilla
  bean, scraped
½ cup heavy cream

1. Combine the chocolate and milk in a saucepan. Heat just to the boiling point, stirring to allow the chocolate to melt.
2. Combine the sugar and eggs in a bowl or mixer and whisk until thick. Gradually whisk in the chocolate mixture.
3. Place in a saucepan and whisk or stir over medium heat until the mixture coats the back of a metal spoon; do not boil.
4. Remove from the heat and stir in the vanilla bean and heavy cream. Transfer to a bowl and place over a larger bowl of ice. Stir until room temperature. Freeze according to manufacturer's directions. Makes 1 quart.

Variation

Add 2–3 tablespoons rum or 4 tablespoons strong espresso coffee to the room-temperature mixture. Add ½ cup chopped and toasted hazelnuts to the room-temperature chocolate or espresso coffee mixture.

Lemon Ice or Granita

Granitas are usually made in a metal tray or bowl and partly frozen, removed from the freezer, beaten with a fork, put back in the freezer until almost solid. The mixture is scraped into glasses and eaten with a spoon and maybe a straw.

3 cups water	Grated rind of 1 lemon
¾ to 1 cup sugar	1 cup fresh lemon juice

Bring the water and sugar to a boil in a saucepan. Cook on low heat for 5 minutes. Cool over ice. Add the rind and juice. Freeze until mushy. Makes 1 quart.

Note: Pour a tablespoon or more of Grappa over each serving. Delicious!

Variation

Coffee ice. Replace the fruit juice and water with strong espresso coffee. Omit the lemon rind.

Pine Nut Tart

2 eggs	1½ cups toasted pine
3 egg yolks	nuts, ground (see
6 tablespoons sugar	note)
1½ cups light cream	Partly baked pastry
½ teaspoon grated	crust (see following
nutmeg	recipe)

1. Beat the eggs, egg yolks, and sugar with a whisk to mix. Add the cream and nutmeg and continue to whisk. Whisk in the pine nuts.
2. Pour into the partly baked pastry shell. Place in a 350-degree oven and bake 20–25 minutes, or until set. Serves 6.

Note: To toast pine nuts, lay them on a baking sheet and bake in a 350-degree oven for 10 minutes. Grind in a blender or food processor. The cooked tart could be cooled to room temperature and served with rosettes of sweetened whipped cream—½ cup heavy cream whipped to soft peaks with 1½ tablespoons confectioners' sugar.

Pastry Crust

2 cups flour
2 tablespoons sugar
12 tablespoons butter,
   cut into small pieces

2 egg yolks
2–3 tablespoons ice
   water

1. Put the flour and sugar in a bowl. Blend in the butter with the fingertips, pastry blender, or two knives. Add the yolks and water and mix. The dough will be sticky.
2. Turn out onto a lightly floured board and knead for a few seconds to smooth. Wrap in foil or plastic and chill in the freezer 10–15 minutes.
3. Roll out the dough until ⅛ inch thick. Fit into a 9-inch tart pan or springform. Prick the pastry with a fork and bake at 350 degrees for 10 minutes. The crust is ready to fill and continue baking. Or cook the crust until light brown and crispy and fill with fruit in season. Brush with fruit glaze and serve.

11

MENUS

Roast loin of veal   172

Sautéed dandelion greens   39

Fresh figs in wine   203

Gloria's chicken with bay leaves   190

Parmesan potatoes   58

Fruit with broiled zabaglione   215–16

Rolled veal scallops   169

Grilled radicchio   60

Mixed fruit   200

Meatballs and mushrooms   177
Baked roasted peppers   56
Ricotta with coffee   214

Minute steaks with olives   174
Baked Spinach   65,66
Selection of cheeses

Veal roll   171
Jean's eggplant   48
Fresh strawberries with vinegar   199

Deviled chicken   192
Fennel with Parmesan cheese   50
Grapes with vanilla sauce   203

Pork chops alla Santina   180
Zucchini with garlic   64
Pears stuffed with Gorgonzola   207

Breaded lamb   186
Stuffed mushrooms   51
Figs in cocoa   202

Fish baked in salt   149

Broccoli with ripe olives   40

Lemon ice with Grappa   219

———————

Scampi   158

Stuffed artichokes   38

Coffee ice   220

———————

Shrimp, potato, and egg salad   21

Fruit and cheese

———————

Baked oysters with pesto   156

Sautéed eggplant Parmesan   44

Lemon ice   219–20

———————

Stuffed small fish   152

Celery with Parmesan   50

Gorgonzola and ripe pears

———————

Chicken Mario   191

Eggplant rolls   45–6

Zabaglione   215

———————

Sausage, onion, and mushroom
custard   182

Escarole   49

Cantaloupe with fruit   200

————————

Fried squid   162

Baked spinach   65, 66

Peaches in Marsala   206

————————

Tuna sauce with chicken   162

Tomatoes stuffed with
rice   62

Bowl of fresh fruit

————————

Veal with mushrooms   173

Fried peppers   55

Baked fresh peaches   204

————————

Swordfish with caper butter   151

Zucchini custards   63

Nectarines with champagne   204

————————

Meat-stuffed zucchini   179

Italian green beans   40

Creamy ricotta dessert   214

————————

Pepper and sausage bake   181

Fennel with oil and lemon   17

Caramelized cherries   200

––––––––––

Baked fish with olives   148

Basil custards   39

Bowl of cherries

––––––––––

Baby lamb chops with
gremolata   185

Celery with toasted pine nuts   48

Stuffed pears   207

––––––––––

Baked fish fillets with
blood oranges   150

Spinach with garlic   66

Amaretto cream   217

––––––––––

Calf's liver, Venice style   184

Zucchini fritters   63

Fresh peaches with Prosecco   206

––––––––––

Shrimp with green sauce   159

Mixed fruit   200

––––––––––

Veal patties with capers   172

Onions with espresso coffee   54

Chocolate almonds   211

———————

Codfish and vermouth   154

Cauliflower with anchovy butter   42

Coffee ice   220

———————

Pasta with lemon sauce   118

Chicken hunter's style · 189

Fresh plums

———————

Chicken strips with sage   188

Peas with ham   52

Fresh figs

———————

Roasted Italian sausage   183

Onions steamed in Chianti   54

Ricotta cake   214

———————

Pasta with butter and
marjoram sauce   111

Shrimp Portofino style   157

Fresh fruit bowl

———————

Turkey breast with basil
cream sauce 195

Mushrooms with Marsala   51

Chocolate ice cream   219

———————

Steak with Marsala   176

Potato croquettes   59

Pine nut tart   220

———————

Tomatoes filled with
rice salad   25

Chicken breasts with sausage   187

Fresh melon slices

———————

Pasta with red clam sauce   110

Pork chops with peppers   181

Lemon ice   219

———————

Pasta with raw tomato
sauce   104

Stuffed eggplant   47

Fruit ice cream   218

———————

Risotto with fresh asparagus
tips   126

Cornish hens in Marsala   196

Vanilla ice cream with Amaretto
chocolate sauce   217, 218

Braciole   175

Italian green beans   40

Bananas baked in Marsala   201

Eggplant soup   72

Prosciutto soufflé   142

Amaretti ice cream   218

Batter-fried chicken   192

Stewed sliced peppers   52

Pears in Marsala   206

Veal scaloppine   170

Eggplant boats   43

Fresh pears

Lasagne   94

Radicchio and fennel salad   30

Nectarines with Prosecco   206

Pasta with broccoli and goat
cheese sauce   116

Veal steak with lemon   168

Figs in cocoa   202

———————

Roasted peppers   55

Veal Parmesan, American-style   166

Fennel with oil and lemon   17

Ice cream with Amaretto
chocolate sauce   217

———————

Spaghetti with tomato sauce   102, 103

Broiled Italian sausage   183

Escarole   49

Mixed fresh fruit

———————

Roast chicken with rosemary   193

Potatoes with peppers   57

Cherries in Chianti   202

———————

Salad Valentino   22

Roasted squabs with
sage butter   197

Broiled polenta   131

Peach and plum compote   205

———————

Veal Marsala   174

Grilled plum tomatoes   61

Bowl of fresh peaches

12

ITALIAN-AMERICAN

AMERICANS LOVE ITALIAN FOOD, AND WE LOVE TO TINKER with the recipes, too. We tinker so much that there are now, in fact, two different styles of cooking "Italian food."

What could be more Italian to most Americans than veal Parmesan? But you will rarely find it in Italy, except in a restaurant that is so Americanized that it serves foreign food. Veal Parmesan was invented in America by Italian immigrants who took the recipe for eggplant Parmesan and combined it with the cheap and plentiful meat available in this country. I love veal Parmesan, and so do my Italian friends, after they get over the shock.

Spaghetti and meatballs, that once-a-week economy standby of the American kitchen, is another American dish. In Italy you would never get meatballs on a pasta with tomato sauce, but you would get polpettine, small meatballs, with a very light tomato sauce.

Americans' long-cooked tomato sauce, called gravy in many Italian-American families, is completely different from Italy's quick version. I have asked some of my

232

American-Italian friends how their sauce came to be called gravy and was told "It's Italian, I guess." I asked many Italians the same question, and soon discovered that there is no word for gravy in Italian, and they could not imagine why a sauce would be called gravy. There are three different words for sauces in Italy—salsa, sugo, and ragu.

Manicotti, which is ever popular in America, is seldom seen in Italy. It is regional and is occasionally seen in Naples and further south, never in the north.

Pizza "with the works" is American. Italian pizzas have one or two things mixed together in the topping, a bit of mozzarella, basil, and tomato for example. They are six to eight inches across, served individually, unsliced, and always with a knife and fork. You are not supposed to eat pizza with your fingers any more than you would twirl pasta on a spoon. The further west you go in America the more pizza has changed. There is a Midwest and a West Coast version, sometimes called Chicago pizza, which is a deep dish pie filled with stuffings you would never find in Italy. Although it is delicious, it has about as much to do with Italian pizza as flapjacks do with crêpes. In the Far West you will find pizza filled with goat cheese, sun-dried tomatoes, pineapple, and God knows what. Certainly not Italian.

You will usually get a piece of lemon peel with your espresso coffee in America and rarely get an espresso coffee with lemon peel in Italy. Italians are as puzzled about this custom as I am. The only explanation I've heard that makes any sense is that there are lots of lemons in Sicily. There are also lots of Sicilians who came over to this country. And maybe when the Sicilians opened restaurants in America, as a few have done, they put lemon in their coffee. Lemon peel does disguise the bitterness of bad espresso, and maybe that is the other reason. Some restaurant owners have told me, "Our customers expect it."

New American cooks are still introducing new "Italian" dishes. A friend of mine defines California cooking

as anything grilled over mesquite, flavored with cilantro,
and splashed with raspberry vinegar. True enough. But
on my last visit to the West Coast, California cooking
seemed to have grown—to include any odd combination
of foods you can imagine served tossed with freshly made
pasta, anything stuffed into ravioli or spread on top of a
pizza. I was even given a recipe for fettuccine with a
peanut butter sauce, which I will never try, even if I do
have the time.

Pasta primavera started in New York City—two different chefs at two different restaurants claim to have
been the first to have the idea. The idea of fresh springtime
vegetables (primavera means spring) finely chopped and
served on spaghetti would be great. But made with broccoli, cauliflower, and winter carrots, it should be called
pasta inverno (the word for winter). Next I expect to see
it made with turnips and rutabagas. The chic pasta to use
for pasta primavera is angel hair, which in Italy is usually
given to the ill or put into soup.

Experimental ravioli is the rage in California right now,
but I was introduced to ravioli stuffed with truffles fifteen
years ago in the south of France. Someone asked the chef
what ravioli was doing in France and he waved grandly
and replied that the Mediterranean extended from Italy
to France and so did cookery. The ravioli, of course, were
wonderful.

I have now seen ravioli stuffed with lobster, American
caviar, and smoked salmon on menus in America, and
even in France. Which must somehow prove that the
Mediterranean extends to Los Angeles and back to Paris—
or at least the food fads do.

Sun-dried tomatoes are appearing more and more in
restaurants, usually as an elegant antipasto, sometimes
sitting on a plate with a few slices of lightly smoked mozzarella or grilled goat cheese. Sun-dried tomatoes are Italian all right, but they are not as popular in restaurants in
Italy as they are in America. In the south of Italy tomatoes
are festooned, like peppers, and hung outside to dry in

the sun. They are used in the winter to perk up a sauce or to be soaked in olive oil and eaten with good country bread. Serving them in an expensive restaurant seems a little odd, but sun-dried tomatoes do taste good, even with slices of smoked mozzarella, or broiled goat cheese.

Cold pasta salads seem to have come first from Chinese cooking, but they were quickly adapted by the mix-and-match school of inventive cooking. Some are good. In Italy, many pastas are tossed warm with raw vegetables and olive oil and served at room temperature. I like these warm pasta salads the best. Of course, Americans have been eating cold pasta salad for years—we called it macaroni salad. Macaroni salad is even less Italian than pasta salad. I remember a chef from Milan, in a discussion of horrible meals, mentioning with particular bitterness that in Switzerland, "where they know nothing about Italian cooking," he was served a pasta salad, "cold as ice and, listen to me, horrible! It had . . . it had mayonnaise . . . on pasta!!!"

I made a note never to serve him macaroni salad, though it is one of my favorite family recipes. Maybe a lot of the Italian food we serve in America tastes good to us only because we are not prejudiced by having eaten the food of Italy.

INDEX

About the Author

JULIE DANNENBAUM is the founder of Creative Cooking in Philadelphia, one of America's most prestigious and successful cooking schools. She also teaches cooking at Venice's Gritti Palace and at the Greenbrier Hotel in White Sulphur Springs, West Virginia. Her previous books include JULIE DANNENBAUM'S CREATIVE COOKING SCHOOL, MENUS FOR ALL OCCASIONS, FAST & FRESH, and MORE FAST & FRESH.

FEAST TO YOUR HEART'S DELIGHT!
BALLANTINE'S
COOKIN' GOOD!